GREAT TASTES OF LONG ISLAND

*Recipes from Favorite Chefs and Restaurants
from The Gold Coast to The Hamptons*

GREAT TASTES OF LONG ISLAND

*Recipes from Favorite Chefs and Restaurants
from The Gold Coast to The Hamptons*

Compiled by
Suffolk AHRC
(ASSOCIATION FOR THE HELP OF RETARDED CHILDREN - Suffolk Chapter)

with wine recommendations from

Ann Marie Borghese
CASTELLO di BORGHESE VINEYARD & WINERY
Cutchogue, NY

Published and Assembled by

2900 Veterans Memorial Highway
Bohemia, NY 11716-1193
www.ahrcsuffolk.org

Publisher: NYSARC, Inc. - Suffolk County Chapter a/k/a
Association for the Help of Retarded Children - Suffolk Chapter (Suffolk AHRC)
2900 Veterans Memorial Highway, Bohemia, NY 11716-1193

Printed on Long Island, NY

Cover & Dividers designed by Pace Advertising Agency, Inc., NYC

ISBN 0-9760267-0-8

The recipes in this collection were submitted by each restaurant's chef. While we cannot guarantee the results, we hope you enjoy reproducing them in your kitchen. Bon Appétit!

Acknowledgments

This cookbook was the endeavor of many people who are committed to expanding opportunities for individuals with developmental challenges. They generously contributed their time, talent, and resources to see that this book came to fruition.

We are indebted to all the wonderful chefs and restaurateurs for their recipes. Without them, there would be no book.

We also want to thank: AT&T for marketing the book through inserts in their household customer account statements; Edward W. Carter of Carter Marketing Group, for donating his talent and creating the marketing material; Gregg Praetorius of Pace Advertising Agency, Inc. for contributing the cover and divider designs as well as his guidance with this project; Ann Marie Borghese of Castello di Borghese Vineyard & Winery for offering her wine selection for each recipe as well as her promotional activities; Cookbook Committee Members: Jay Andreassi, Marc Blitstein, Duffy Mich, Frank Filipo, Eileen Fleischer, Beverly Geiger, Joe Mammolito, Sean Rose and Ken Walker for all their hard work.

Duffy Mich of Intelecom Systems, Inc. deserves a very special thank you. Duffy conceived the idea and facilitated its production.

Thank you to the AHRC staff for undertaking the challenge of this project and to all the volunteers who contributed to getting their favorite restaurants to participate.

Lastly, but perhaps most importantly, thank you to everyone who purchases this book. In doing so, you are providing pathways to opportunities for people with developmental challenges.

WHY THIS COOKBOOK?

Why would a not-for-profit organization whose mission is to maximize the quality of life for children and adults with developmental disabilities be in the cookbook business?

The answer is WORK. The successful sale of this book will create ongoing work for more than 600 adults who attend a Vocational Training Center operated by the AHRC (Association for the Help of Retarded Children), Suffolk Chapter. Jobs associated with the production of this cookbook such as collating, binding, packaging and mailing are handled at one of three Suffolk County, NY Work Centers, by groups of adults, under the close supervision of their instructors.

For more than thirty years, AHRC has partnered with the business community. As a packaging and assembly sub-contractor, AHRC offers businesses, large and small, an alternative to outsourcing work overseas. This relationship results in vocational training opportunities for the adults in the three work centers.

The cookbook is yet another contract for this program - the only difference is that this contract is being awarded by the organization itself. To speak with a business representative for information on outsourcing work to AHRC call (631) 585-0100.

Dedicated to the men and women who benefit from the vocational training opportunities they receive at Suffolk AHRC Work Centers

ABOUT CASTELLO DI BORGHESE VINEYARD AND WINERY

A new era began when my husband and I opened Castello di Borghese Vineyard and Winery on the founding Long Island wine estate planted in 1973. We began making our mark in the wine industry with true passion and determination.

Marco and Ann Marie Borghese

Castello di Borghese is nestled in the beautiful North Fork town of Cutchogue which is blessed with a 210 day growing season and sandy loam soil. Our vines are of the most mature and produce wines that are sophisticated, elegant and critically-acclaimed.

The region celebrated the 30th anniversary with a grand gala at Castello di Borghese. Today there are 55 vineyards and 31 wineries attracting many tourists and wine enthusiasts. The Long Island wine community helps sustain the natural charm of the East End from over development and puts forth a bounty of local product while protecting the environment.

My family's dedication, together with our winemaker Mark Terry, to the art of fine wine making is enhanced by our involvement with other art forms. A visit to our tasting room will showcase many varietals of wines and two galleries for ongoing exhibitions, operas, book signings and other cultural events presented for the enjoyment of our friends in the Long Island community.

A while ago I had the pleasure of meeting AHRC's Executive Director, Joe Mammolito at a local art exhibit. In conversation, Joe mentioned this cookbook and invited me to participate by offering suggestions of wines to complement the recipes. It is, indeed, an honor and a pleasure to be part of this very special project. I hope you find my suggestions and comments helpful and interesting.

Bon Appetit,

Princess Ann Marie Borghese

CASTELLO di BORGHESE

**P.O. Box 957
Cutchogue, NY 11935
Tel. 631-734-5111 Fax 631-734-5485
www.castellodiborghese.com**

CONTENTS

Had *Great Tastes of Long Island* been a standard cookbook, it might have been valuable as a listing of favorite recipes from the kitchens of notable Long Island chefs. But now Princess Ann Marie Borghese has presented something more. Drawing on the handsome wines made at the Castello di Borghese family vineyard, and on her keen sense of their subtleties, she has supplied original and exciting ideas about food-and-wine pairing. She has effectively demolished the mythology surrounding that deceptively familiar discipline.

Just as the value of great music rests in notes and what's done with them, Ann Marie understands how a "note" of flavor in a great wine unlocks the taste of fine food. Again and again, she shows that the only rules that govern are those of a diner's individual preference. When she recommends Castello di Borghese Founder's Field Sauvignon Blanc Reserve, for example, to go with Chef Scott Szekretar's sesame tuna, she does so with understanding of how this fine wine's back-flavors of mango, honeysuckle, melon and tropical fruit can coax new levels of taste out of a choice entree.

When she and her husband, Italian Prince Marco Borghese, purchased the founding vineyard of the Long Island wine industry in 1999, the North Fork of Long Island was already a well-established wine destination. Hugh Johnson and Jancis Robinson enthusiastically termed it "New York's answer to Bordeaux." But the Borgheses haven't stopped there. If they have their way -- and there's no reason to believe they won't -- people everywhere will soon recognize and revere the excellence of their Long Island vintages.

The recipes included here are all first-rate, supplied by the best chefs of Long Island. The wines, all Castello di Borghese specialties, will surprise and delight you, as they did me, with their subtleties and secrets. In every sense this is a book to treasure; a guide to successful mating of excellent wine with finely prepared food. For me, as well as for you, it's a volume which should give many hours of satisfaction.

Richard M. Sudhalter

Mr. Studhalter, a prominent jazz cornetist, is the author of STARDUST MELODY: The Life and Music of Hoagy Carmichael

Participating Restaurants

APPETIZERS

appetizers

105 HARBOR

NEW AMERICAN CUISINE
STEAKS, SEAFOOD, RAW BAR, MARTINIS

105 Harbor Road
Cold Spring Harbor

Phone: 631-367-3166
www.105Harbor.com

John Brill, Executive Chef

Attire: Casual Neat
Reservations Recommended
AmEx, Visa, Master Card, Diner's Club

LUNCH
Monday - Saturday 11:30 am - 3:00 pm

DINNER
Monday - Thursday 5:00 pm - 9:30 pm
Friday - Saturday 5:00 pm - 10:30 pm
Sunday 5:00 pm - 9:00 pm

BRUNCH
Sunday 11:30 am - 3:30 pm

Situated in a 17th century building that used to serve as a hotel, 105 Harbor is a romantic restaurant located on the North Shore. The chef has assembled distinctive menus offering culinary delights, creatively plated to enhance the dining experience.

Whether you sample from the Lunch, Dinner, Brunch or Dessert menus, you'll find it difficult to choose from their vast and internationally inspired array of tempting seafood, steaks, pastas and desserts. Savor the chef's creations accompanied by fine wines while enjoying breathtaking views of the harbor.

tuna tartare with micro green salad and wasabi ginger lime vinaigrette

Serves: 2

Tuna Tartare
4 ounces sushi-grade yellowfin tuna, well chilled
2 tablespoons chives, finely chopped
1 tablespoon pickled ginger, finely chopped
1 ounce wasabi ginger lime vinaigrette

Coarse salt and Japanese five pepper togarshmi, to taste

Micro Herb Salad
Baby frisée, small head
¼ cup micro pepper cress
¼ cup micro arugula
¼ cup micro red cabbage
2 tablespoons wasabi ginger lime vinaigrette

To prepare tuna, work quickly, dice tuna into ¼ inch pieces. Cover and refrigerate until ready to use. Just before serving, mix the tuna, chives, pickled ginger and vinaigrette. Season with coarse salt and Japanese pepper.

Wasabi Ginger Lime Vinaigrette
Mix together: 2 ounces freshly squeezed lime juice
1 tablespoon white truffle oil
1 ounce wasabi
1 ounce yuzu citrus juice (optional)

Presentation
Combine salad ingredients with the vinaigrette. On the center of each serving plate, spoon the tuna tartare into a 2 ½ inch x 1 ½ inch round metal mold, flattening the top. Remove the mold. Top the tartare with the salad and serve.

Two wines come to mind, Castello di Borghese Riesling and the Founder's Field Sauvignon Blanc. Both have beautiful fruit, floral aroma and softness like honey in your mouth. The Riesling has a bit of a tangy sensation.

Aix

en-Provence

134 NEW YORK AVENUE, HUNTINGTON

TEL: 631-549-3338 / FAX: 631-549-2542

Mitchell Hauser, Chef

French American Cuisine

Open for dinner at 5:00 pm every night, except Mondays

Visa, Master Card, and AmEx Accepted

www.aixenprovencehuntington.com

Located in picturesque Huntington Harbor, this French American restaurant features a menu that is a mixture of French Classics and some American versions. The atmosphere is simple country French with cream colored table linens topped with subtle tuile table lamps, and open, airy, and inviting French doors leading to outside patio dining under a canopy in the warmer months. At Aix they strive to provide the ultimate combination of superb atmosphere, food, and wine service. It is a destination restaurant worthy of a trip off the beaten path.

roasted garlic crusted shrimp

Serves: 8 (4 shrimp per person)

32 large shrimp, peeled and deveined
50 cloves garlic, peeled
1 cup blended oil

16 wood skewers
2 cups Panko (*Japanese breadcrumbs*)

Salt and pepper to taste

Place garlic in small ovenproof pot and cover with oil.
Slow cook at 300°F in oven for 1 hour.
Remove and strain (saving oil). Purée garlic in food processor.

For each serving, take 2 skewers and skewer 4 shrimp tightly together.
Season with salt and pepper.

Spread garlic purée over shrimp and dredge in breadcrumbs.
Sauté in reserved oil until browned on both sides.
Finish in oven if necessary.

Serve over salad or with pasta.

Chef's Note: This crust works with lobster, chicken and even skewered asparagus.

Editor's Note: This recipe really does call for 50 cloves of garlic!

Perfect with Castello di Borghese Estate Chardonnay.

**21 FIRE ISLAND AVENUE
BABYLON VILLAGE**

Tel: 631-422-5161 / Fax: 631-422-5097

CHRISTOPHER CUTLER, *Executive Chef*

Continental Bistro Menu

HOURS
Monday - Friday 11:30 am - 11:00 pm
Saturday 5:00 pm - 11:00 pm
Sunday 4:00 pm - 10:00 pm

Neat Casual Attire

Visa, MC, AmEx, Diner's Cards Accepted

Executive Chef, Chris Cutler, has been honing his expertise for the past 20 years on Long Island. During that time he spent the last 16 years as proprietor and executive chef at Mims Restaurants in Roslyn and Syosset. Now Chris Cutler is getting rave reviews as the executive chef at the Babylon Carriage House.

appetizers 8

buffalo chicken and sonoma cheddar spring rolls

Serves: 1

1 6-ounce chicken breast, fried

2 ounces cheddar cheese, diced

1 teaspoon sliced scallion

1 tablespoon hot sauce

2 spring roll wrappers

1 egg (for wash)

Dice fried chicken; combine all ingredients in a mixing bowl except spring roll.

Put mixture on spring roll, use an eggwash to seal spring roll wrapper.

Makes 2 rolls.

Fry for 3-4 minutes at 350°F.

Serve with bleu cheese dressing.

 Try Castello di Borghese Cabernet Franc with this appetizer.

55 Main Street, Cold Spring Harbor

Tel: 631-692-5655 / Fax: 516-422-3900

Kevin and Karen Peck, Owners
Hal Goldman, Chef

New American/Seafood Cuisine

Credit Cards: Visa, MC, AmEx

Reservations recommended Friday - Sunday

Open 7 Days

Sunday - Thursday: 11:00 am - 10:00 pm
Friday and Saturday: 11:00 am - 11:00 pm

This old-fashioned, upscale gem is North Shore sophistication at its best with a friendly and intimate atmosphere.The menu at this elegant fish house revolves around the freshest seafood. The dining room is elegant and uncomplicated; at lunch time enjoy a mix of salads and wraps while sitting at one of the outside tables.

Children are most welcome.

corn fried oysters with dijon aioli and lemon jam

Serves: 4

16 oysters (shucked)
2 cups flour
1 cup corn meal
Salt and pepper, to taste
Old Bay Seasoning,
   to taste
Cayenne pepper, to taste

Lemon Jam
3 lemons
1 ½ cups sugar
¼ cup lemon juice
2 tablespoons olive oil

Dijon Aioli
2 cups mayonnaise
1 ½ tablespoons black
   pepper
½ cup Dijon mustard

Shuck oysters and reserve shells (bottom only). Combine flour and corn meal. Season with salt, pepper, Old Bay Seasoning and cayenne pepper all to taste. Dredge oysters in flour mix and fry to golden brown.

Lemon Jam
Cut lemons in small pieces. Remove seeds. Place in food processor and blend until smooth. Add sugar and lemon juice. While machine is on, drizzle in olive oil.

Dijon Aioli
Combine mayonnaise, black pepper and mustard. Mix well.

Presentation
Place 4 oyster shells on plate. Put 1 teaspoon lemon jam on inside of shell. Place oyster on top of jam. Drizzle plate with Dijon aioli.

Chef's Note: Serve with cole slaw. It is a great dish to serve at dinner parties or barbecues in the summertime.

 Castello di Borgese Riesling turns this summertime dish into a fiesta. So celebrate!

114 Broadhollow Road, Melville

Tel: 631-385-7380 / Fax: 631-385-0912

Dean Cirella, Chef/Owner

All major credit cards accepted

casual, neat attire

<u>Hours</u>
Monday - Thursday: 11:30 am - 10:00 pm
Friday: 11:30 am - 11:00 pm
Saturday: 5:00 pm - 11:00 pm
Sunday: 4:00 pm - 9:00 pm

Enjoy Cirella's contemporary ambiance, quick, friendly service with a smile and consistently good food. Owned and operated by two generations of the Cirella family, the authentic Italian menu offers Cirella's variations of traditional dishes that you rarely experience at other "Italian" restaurants.

"Our Family Serving yours for Over 16 Years."

portobello nape

Serves: 4

4 Portobello mushrooms (4 inches) clean and cut stems. Oven roast for 15 minutes at 450°F

1 grilled red pepper, fire roast and peel, cut into quarters

1 10-ounce ball of fresh mozzarella, sliced ½ inch thick

6 cups balsamic vinegar, cook in sauce pot for 30 minutes at boil temperature

1 stick of butter (add to balsamic while boiling to thicken sauce)

On a sheet pan, layer the Portobello mushrooms, roasted red pepper and the mozzarella. Bake in oven at 450°F (10 - 12 minutes). When mozzarella starts to cool down, item is done.

Drizzle balsamic nape onto plate. Slide Portobello stack onto nape.

Garnish with fresh basil for color.

Enjoy!

Chef's Note: We serve it as an appetizer. It's fast, easy, colorful, and tasty. It looks like the Leaning Tower of Pisa.

Relatively unknown as a varietal, Cabernet Franc is a full flavored wine with hints of tobacco and enhanced by blackberry and cherry notes. It is a great food wine but also wonderful by the glass.

CITTANUOVA

Contemporary Regional Italian Food

29 Newtown Lane, East Hampton
Tel: 631-324-6300 / Fax: 631-324-9537

www.cittanuova.com

JAMES GEE, CHEF

Open Monday - Friday
Lunch: 11:30 am - 4:00 pm
Dinner: 5:00 pm - 11:30 pm

Reservations required for parties of 8 or more

Casual Attire

Visa, MC, AmEx Accepted

Cittanuova is a contemporary Italian restaurant nestled in the heart of East Hampton village. Located in the former space of The Grill, at 29 Newtown Lane, Cittanuova - Italian for "New Town" - is named for the street that the restaurant fronts.

The menu focuses on traditional Italian dishes with a nod to locally grown seasonal produce, accompanied by a small, but well-chosen wine list featuring only Italian and Long Island labels.

During the warm weather, the façade's retractable pocket doors open completely while al fresco dining is available in a lush enclosed garden behind the restaurant and on Newtown Lane.

eggplant caponata with crostini

2 large eggplants
2 red bell peppers, large dice
1 red onion, medium dice
1 medium carrot, medium dice
1 stalk celery, medium dice
4 cloves garlic, crushed

2 ounces capers
2 ounces golden raisins
1 cup white wine
1 cup red wine vinegar
2 sprigs fresh marjoram
8 ounce can Italian peeled tomatoes
¼ cup sugar
1 cup pine nuts, lightly toasted

½ cup extra virgin olive oil
¼ tablespoon crushed red pepper
1 tablespoon kosher salt and pepper to taste
1 large ciabatta bread or baguette
Olive oil for brushing

Slice and salt the eggplant and let sit for 20 minutes. Meanwhile, in a heavy bottom skillet, add olive oil and garlic. Sauté, do not brown. Add onion, carrots, celery, bell peppers, crushed red pepper and salt. Cover and sweat over medium low heat.

Rinse eggplant and pat dry. Cut into medium dice and add to the pan.
Cover and cook for 10 additional minutes. Deglaze with white wine and vinegar. Add sugar, capers, marjoram and raisins.

Puree the tomatoes and add to the pan. Cover and simmer on low for 30 minutes.

Taste for seasoning. Add pine nuts and transfer to suitable dish to refrigerate. Chill at least 3 hours or overnight.

Before serving, slice bread to approximately 1 inch thick, brush with olive oil and season with salt. Over a fire grill, lightly char the bread on both sides. You can also toast the bread in a very hot oven until lightly toasted but soft on the inside.

Serve immediately with caponata.

Chef's Note: Can be made a day prior and kept chilled.

 Depending on how rich or full-bodied you want your wine to be, try either Castello di Borghese Merlot or Merlot Reserve. Our Merlot is a good example of North Fork Terroir.

EAST BY NORTHEAST

51 SOUTH EDGEMERE STREET, MONTAUK

Tel: 631-668-2872 / Fax: 631-668-7052

www.harvest2000.com

BRUCE BERNACCHIA AND JOHN ERB, OWNERS
ANTHONY SILVESTRI, CHEF

casual but neat attire

Visa and Mastercard accepted

Hours:
Weekdays in season/5:00 pm - 10:00 pm
Friday and Saturday in season/5:00 pm - 11:00 pm

Reservations required 1 week in advance

East by Northeast is a culinary journey from the Far East to the Northeast.
Chef Anthony Silvestri creates amazing presentations from a menu that includes Montauk
favorites as well as flavors from across the Far East.

Panoramic views of Fort Pond, our newly renovated dining room, stone wine room, and
comfortable bar and lounge make ENE perfect for a casual dinner or any special occasion.

roasted diver sea scallops with mangoes, thai chilies, cashews

Serves: 6

12 sea scallops,
muscle removed
2 tablespoons ginger,
peeled and minced
2 tablespoons garlic,
minced
1 teaspoon Thai chilies,
minced fine
1 cup salted cashew nuts

1 cup ripe mango,
peeled, seeded and
diced small
1 cup red pepper,
diced small
1 cup mango broth
4 tablespoons scallions,
sliced
3 tablespoons butter
Salt and pepper
Sesame seeds for garnish

Mango Broth
2 carrots, chopped
2 stalks of celery, chopped
1/2 of onion, chopped
4 cups chicken broth
1 cup mango puree

To make the mango broth, place a medium size sauce pan on the stove and sweat the vegetables in a little oil for about two minutes. Add the chicken stock and mango puree and simmer for about 30 minutes. Season with salt and pepper and strain, keep in a warm place.

To complete the dish, heat a medium size sauté pan on medium heat. Add a little oil and place the scallops in the pan and season them with salt and pepper. Sear on one side and turn them over and place them into a 350°F degree oven for two minutes. Take them out of the oven and let them rest. In the same pan, sauté the ginger, garlic, Thai chilies, red peppers, mango broth and mangoes until translucent in color. Add the rest of the ingredients and reduce the sauce until it slightly thickens and season with salt and pepper.

Place the scallops on the plate and pour the sauce on top of the scallops. Garnish with chopped scallions and sesame seeds.

Chef's Note: This is a great summer dish with fresh ingredients!

Quick! Open a bottle of Castello di Borghese Riesling. The Thai chilies will be so happy once they are awash with our Riesling; so will the diver scallops.

720 Main Road
Aquebogue

New American Cuisine

Phone: 631-722-5813
www.FaunaRestaurant.com

Robert Mittleman, Mark Mittleman and Bobby Mittleman, Owners
Mark Mittleman, Executive Chef

Attire: Smart Casual
Reservations Recommended

HOURS:
Summer/Fall
Lunch
Sunday - Thursday Noon - 4:00 pm
Dinner
Sunday - Thursday 5:00 pm - 9:00 pm
Friday and Saturday 5:00 pm - 10:00 pm

A North Fork restaurant and full-service caterer located in the gateway to Long Island wine country, Fauna is a savory restaurant where the atmosphere is relaxed and the menu diverse.

Using fresh local products whenever possible, the chef incorporates international flavors, including Italian, Mediterranean, Asian and Middle Eastern elements into dishes to bring a worldly taste to the North Fork.

mushroom tapenade with crostini

1½ pounds of mixed fresh mushrooms (button, Portobello, shiitake, oyster, crimini, etc.)
3 tablespoons extra-virgin olive oil
¼ teaspoon salt
3 cloves garlic, minced

6 anchovy filets
1 tablespoon drained capers
2 teaspoons minced fresh rosemary or thyme
½ - ¾ cup extra-virgin olive oil
Salt and pepper to taste

2 French baguettes - cut on a bias
Extra-virgin olive oil, for drizzling

For the Tapenade
Preheat oven to 425°F. Remove any tough stems from the mushrooms. Toss with the 3 tablespoons of olive oil and salt. Spread out in a single layer onto a baking sheet and roast for 20 minutes. Let cool. Some will be shriveled and this is fine. Place in a food processor with the garlic, anchovies, rosemary or thyme and capers. Pulse until combined. With the motor running add the olive oil in a steady stream to form a juicy paste. Taste and season with salt and pepper. Serve with crostini.
Makes 1 ½ cups.

For the Crostini
Preheat the oven to 425°F. Place sliced baguettes on baking sheet in a single layer. Drizzle extra-virgin olive oil on bread and toast until golden brown. Cool the bread. The crostini can be stored in an airtight container at room temperature for 2 days.

Castello di Borghese recommends Pinot Noir.

INTERMEZZO

Italian Bistro, Bar & Lounge

964 Middle Country Road, St. James

Tel: 631-265-1212 / Fax: 631-265-1515

www.intermezzoli.com

James Gardner and Tara Potthof, Proprietors
Adam Pitre, Executive Chef

Credit cards: Visa, MC, AmEx

casual, neat attire

Hours
Monday - Thursday: 11:00 am - 10:00 pm
Friday and Saturday: 2:00 pm - 2:00 am
Sunday: 11:00 am - 10:00 pm

Reservations for parties of 6 or more

Contemporary and chic describe the venue and the Italian food at Intermezzo. The architecturally designed modern structure is appreciated inside the sophisticated dining room, with its two story ceiling and large windows. The atmosphere is spacious yet intimate.

Chef Adam Pitre creates flavorful dishes with simple ingredients and presents them artistically. There are frequent special events and dancing in the after-hours lounge.

curried diver scallops with a mint mango coulis

Serves: 1

4 diver sea scallops
(approximately ½
pound)
½ cup cooked wild
rice
1 pureed mango (ripe)

Spice mix-blend of 1
teaspoon each:
Cajun spice, curry
powder and cumin
1 can Coco Lopez
(sweet coconut cream)

½ cup heavy cream
1 vanilla bean (de-seeded)
Pinch of fresh mint
1 fried tortilla triangle
(garnish)

In a small sauté pan, heat until smoking point. Dredge scallops with spice mix and sear with a light coating of olive oil, 2 minutes per side. Turn off heat and leave in pan.

In another sauté pan, warm rice and add cream, Coco Lopez (½ can), and vanilla bean and reduce until creamy. Warm mango puree and add mint. Spoon a mold of rice in center of plate, place scallops around, drizzle with mango sauce.

Garnish with chip and sprig of fresh mint.

Chef's Note: Intense flavor, quick preparation, beautiful presentation.

Founder's Field Sauvignon Blanc is the right combination for this intriguing recipe.

Kitchen *a bistro*

532 Route 25A, St. James
631-862-0151

Eric Lomando, Owner and Chef
Robert Mathews, Chef

no credit cards accepted / casual attire

BYOB - no corkage fee

Lunch	*Dinner*
Monday - Thursday Noon - 2:30pm	Monday - Thursday 5:30 pm - 9 pm
Friday Noon - 2pm	Reservations are required
Saturday 11:30 am - 2 pm	Friday - Sunday evenings
Sunday 11:00 am - 1 pm	*No reservations necessary during the week*

Kitchen a Bistro is a small French bistro with a daily changing menu featuring the market's freshest seasonal ingredients.

tar tar of filet mignon

Serves: 4

1 pound filet mignon
   diced by hand
1 shallot, brunoise
   (finely diced)

2 tablespoons chives,
   chopped
4 tablespoons soy sauce
6 tablespoons peanut oil

Combine shallots, chives, filet mignon and season
with course cracked black pepper.

Divide among four dishes.

Heat oil and add soy sauce when oil is hot,
pour over filet mignon and serve immediately
with crispy bread.

*Cabernet Franc is most often used as a blending wine. Castello di Borghese
Cabernet Blanc Reserve is a rich generous wine and has marvelously deep
focused flavors of red berry, blackberry and black tea. A slightly spicy taste; the
Cabernet Franc Reserve has a full mouth-feel and a long lingering finish.*

La Coquille

1669 NORTHERN BOULEVARD
MANHASSET

516-365-8422

www.lacoquillemanhasset.com

- FRENCH SEAFOOD -

Reservations Requested

All Major Cards Accepted

PASQUALE VENEZIANO, OWNER
AMERICO MINTEGO, CHEF

Open 7 Days
Dinner
5:30 pm - Closing
Sunday 5:00 pm - 9:00 pm

Jackets Suggested

A landmark in Manhasset, La Coquille maintains the tradition of offering the finest classical French cuisine in an elegant and romantic setting. The atmosphere is relaxed and comfortable. The extensive menu, which is true to its original French heritage, offers house specialties which include foie gras, sweet breads and giant Beluga caviar. The signature dish is Long Island Duckling a L'Orange. They feature over 12 different seafood entrées every night.

La Coquille stands out on Long Island as one of the few classic French restaurants, with an established reputation for fine food and excellent service.

escargots bourguignons

Serves: 2

8 cloves of garlic
(blanched and pureed)
1 whole shallot
(chopped)
½ bunch flat leaf parsley
(chopped fine)
1 ounce brandy

1 ounce white wine
4 ounces soft butter
12 fresh escargot in
shell (canned can be
substituted)
1 whole bay leaf

15 whole black
peppercorns
2 sprigs fresh thyme
½ sliced onion (yellow)
1 stalk celery (sliced)
½ carrot (sliced)

For the Compound Butter
In a stand mixer, whip butter to double in volume. Add shallot, garlic and parsley.
Add brandy and white wine until incorporated. Set aside to cool and refrigerate.

For the Escargot
In a pot of cold water (2 quarts), place bay leaf, peppercorns, thyme, onion, celery and
carrot. Add escargot and bring to a simmer. If dealing with the live escargot, salt the
sides of the pot to avoid escargot escaping. Drain, cool, and with a toothpick pull the
escargot out of shell. (If dealing with canned escargot, just simply rinse and drain.)

Assembly
Clean and rinse shells. Fill ½ the shells with compound butter, then 1 escargot and
finish stuffing the shells with more butter. Place in a preheated oven at 350°F on a
baking sheet for 6-10 minutes or until brown and bubbly. Do not allow butter to
break in oven. Serve with French bread. Enjoy!

The compound butter can be made up to one week ahead of time. Please do not
freeze and assemble on the moment.

*Chef's Note: This dish is made for dipping. Crunchy, rustic French bread with the herbed
garlic butter is a must.*

*Depending on when this course is being served, pair earlier in a meal with
Castello di Borghese Barrel Fermented Chardonnay or later in the meal with
Castello di Borghese Merlot.*

Monica Bella

Cucina Italiana

315 Walt Whitman Road
Huntington Station

631-549-3033

ANTHONY AND MONICA FRASCONE, OWNERS
NORBERTO AVILLA, CHEF

AMEX, VISA, Master Card, Discover

Hours
Lunch
Monday - Saturday
Noon - 4:00 pm

Dinner
Monday - Thursday 4:00 pm - 10:00 pm
Friday - Saturday 4:00 pm - 11:30 pm
Sunday 4:00 pm - 9:00 pm

Attire: Casual Neat

The place for fine dining without the attitude. A casual and comfortable atmosphere, with exceptional food and service, rated "excellent" on the 2004-2005 Zagat Dining guide.

mozzarella napoletana

Serves: 4

1 pound fresh mozzarella cheese, sliced medium thick

2 ½ medium to large Holland or beefsteak tomatoes, sliced medium thick widthwise

3 whole red peppers, sliced

3 large Portobello mushrooms, baked

1 small red onion, diced and fully cooked

4 ounces sun-dried tomatoes

8 ounces balsamic vinegar

Coat whole peppers with olive oil on all sides. Roast peppers under broiler rotating until skin turns black on all sides. When fully cooked remove from heat.
Place in paper bag and seal. Leave in paper bag for 20 minutes, then remove peppers. Remove burnt skin and take out all seeds from inside peppers. Slice peppers ¼ inch lengthwise.

In medium sauce pot heat balsamic vinegar, bring to boil and add red diced onion. Simmer for 20 minutes or until sauce is thick.

Layer one slice of mozzarella, one slice of tomato, one strip of pepper, and 2 pieces of sun-dried tomato. Repeat process one more time.

Take baked Portobello mushrooms and slice lengthwise into ¼ inch thick pieces.
Lay 4 pieces of mushroom on the sides of mozzarella, peppers and tomatoes.
Pour warm balsamic dressing over entire layers of mozzarella and tomatoes.
Garnish with fresh basil.

Enjoy!

 Castello di Borghese Estate Chardonnay and Chef Avilla's recipe are a harmonious pairing. Both have clean distinct characteristics.

PAGE ONE RESTAURANT

**90 SCHOOL STREET
GLEN COVE**

Asian-American Cuisine

Phone: 516-676-2800
Fax: 516-656-0415

www.pageonerestaurant.com

JEANINE DIMENNA AND PETER ANTONOPOULOS, OWNERS
JEANINE DIMENNA, CHEF

ATTIRE: Casual Neat

HOURS:
Lunch
7 days 12:00 pm - 3:00 pm

Dinner
Monday - Thursday 4:30 pm - 10:00 pm
Friday - Sunday 4:30 pm - 11:00 pm

The owners of Page One Restaurant strive to assure that every person who enters leaves with a dining experience they won't soon forget.

pacific wonton wrapped shrimp with ponzu wasabi dipping sauce

Serves: 4 appetizers or 2 entrees

12 shrimp, peeled, deveined and butterflied (size 0-12)
12 6-inch skewers
12 wonton wrappers (3 x 3)
1 egg, beaten
Shallow fry pan
Oil to fill pan ½ way

For Dipping sauce
2 cups soy sauce
½ cup mirin
½ cup lime juice
½ cup sugar
1 tablespoon grated fresh ginger
1 tablespoon horseradish

1 tablespoon wasabi powder
½ cup fresh scallions

Skewer each shrimp (through tail straight to end of shrimp).

Lay wonton wrapper flat on work table. Brush ends with beaten egg. Starting at the end of each wonton, roll up shrimp lengthwise.

Heat oil to 350°F. Add 3 shrimp at a time until golden brown.
Place on paper towel.

Repeat with remaining shrimp.

Dipping Sauce
Take ¼ cup soy sauce, add wasabi powder and make a paste.

With remaining soy sauce, mix mirin, lime juice, sugar, ginger and horseradish.
Mix in wasabi paste.

Slice scallions and stir into ponzu wasabi dipping sauce.

Castello di Borghese Riesling has refreshing pear and peach flavors which blend gloriously with shrimp and spice.

RUVO

Country Italian Cuisine

63 Broadway, Greenlawn
Telephone: 631-261-7700 / Fax: 631-261-7792

www.ruvorestaurant.com

Joseph and James DeNicola, Owners

Wilmer Bedoya, Chef

Hours
Lunch
Monday to Friday: Noon - 3 pm
Dinner
Monday to Thursday: 5 pm - 9:30 pm
Friday and Saturday: 5 pm - 10:30 pm
Sunday: 5 pm - 9 pm

Ruvo is a country Italian restaurant, owned and operated by the DeNicola brothers, serving traditional family recipes along with daily specials, including fresh seafood and homemade desserts.

"A True Trattoria" ~Newsday
"Ruvo offers incredible dishes" ~ NY Times

lump crab cakes over lentil salad with wasabi mayonnaise

Serves: 8

Crab Cakes
2 pounds of jumbo lump
 crab meat
2 egg whites
1 tablespoon Dijon
 mustard
3 tablespoons mayonnaise
1 chopped roasted red
 pepper
1 tablespoon flour
3 cups white bread
 crumbs
1 teaspoon salt and
 pepper
1 teaspoon Italian parsley,
 chopped

2 teaspoons Florida Bay
 seasoning

Lentil Salad
1 pound (1 bag) of
 lentils (pre-soaked for
 1 hour)
1 onion, quartered
2 celery stalks, cut into
 chunks
1 carrot, sliced 1 inch
 thick
2 bay leaves
1 red onion, chopped
1 roasted red pepper,
 chopped

Salt and pepper to taste
½ cup chopped basil
½ cup balsamic vinegar
1 cup olive oil

Wasabi Mayonnaise
1 ½ cups mayonnaise
4 tablespoons wasabi
 powder
½ teaspoon cayenne
 pepper
2 tablespoons lime juice
Salt and pepper to taste

Crab Cakes
In large mixing bowl, combine 1 cup of bread crumbs with remainder of ingredients. Mix to an even consistency. Spread rest of bread crumbs on large platter. Use an ice cream scooper and portion out scoops of crab mixture. Roll portions of crab in balls. Flatten crab in bread crumbs making patties. In large frying pan, sauté cakes in medium-hot vegetable oil until brown on both sides, about 5 minutes. Place on paper towels to absorb oil.

Lentil Salad
Strain and dry lentils. Cook the lentils in 2 quarts of water, together with 1 onion, 2 stalks of celery, 1 carrot and 2 bay leaves. Cook for 20 minutes. Discard the vegetables. Strain and dry the lentils and let them cool. Combine lentils and remaining ingredients and chill.

Wasabi Mayonnaise
Mix all ingredients in large bowl.

Presentation
Put crab cakes on lentil salad. Add wasabi mayonnaise to side of lentil salad and top of crab cakes.

Castello di Borghese Riesling, Sauvignon Blanc or Estate Chardonnay will go with this all time favorite recipe.

The Seafood Barge

62980 Main Road (Rte. 25)
Southold

Seafood

Phone: 631-765-3010
www.seafoodbarge.com

Richard Ehrlich, Owner
Matthew L. Lewis, Executive Chef
John Scunziano, Sous Chef

Reservations Recommended

Casual Neat Attire

VISA, MasterCard, American Express

HOURS:
Monday - Friday Noon - 3 pm Lunch
Monday- Friday 5 pm - 9 pm Dinner
Saturday Noon - 10 pm
Sunday Noon - 9 pm

The Seafood Barge offers great views of the beautiful Peconic Bay from every table. With their casual dress code, crisp linens, and nautical décor, the Seafood Barge is the perfect spot to enjoy a well-prepared meal and a glass of Long Island wine in a relaxed atmosphere.

Join them for lunch or dinner and savor fresh, local seafood, Sushi, and a delicious Raw Bar offering fresh shucked local oysters, Little Neck Clams and shrimp. Superb pasta dishes, herb-crusted roast chicken, roast lamb, and filet mignon assure delicious choices for all guests.

To complement the diverse food choices, the wine list offers over 100 wines, including at least 60 Long Island wines, and a knowledgeable staff is available to suggest delicious wine and food pairings.

lobster spring rolls

Serves: 6

½ pound claw and knuckle lobster meat, rung dry (drained well)*

Spinach Mix:
1 ½ teaspoons butter
1 tablespoon blended oil

1 tablespoon garlic, diced
1 tablespoon shallot, diced
¼ teaspoon red pepper flakes
1 ⅛ teaspoons sesame oil
2 ½ teaspoons sesame seeds

20 ounces cello spinach, cleaned
Salt and pepper to taste
6 spring roll wrappers
1 whole egg, for egg wash

In a rondeau**, put your butter, oil, garlic, shallots and sauté about 4 minutes. Add the fresh spinach and sauté until spinach is wilted. Add remaining ingredients and remove from heat.

Strain the spinach after it cools (drain well). After spinach mixture is chilled, ring dry. Take your spring roll wrappers, lay out flat and place about 1 tablespoon of the spinach mixture and 1 teaspoon of the lobster meat and roll the spring roll putting an egg wash on the corners and wrap tightly.

Deep fry and serve.

Chef's Note: Any lobster will do. Rung dry means well drained.

Editor's Note: A rondeau is a large, round, heavy bottomed, ovenproof, medium-deep pot with two loop handles.

 Pair with Castello di Borghese Estate Chardonnay, an absolute classic.

967 Old Country Road
Westbury

www.tesorosrestaurant.com

Phone: 516-334-0022

ANGELO GIANNUZZI, OWNER/CHEF
ANTONIO VITUCCI, OWNER/MAITRE'D

Casual Neat Attire

HOURS:
Tuesday - Thursday 11:00 am - 10:00 pm
Friday 11:00 am - 11:00 pm
Saturday 2:00 pm - 11:00 pm
Sunday 2:00 pm - 10:00 pm
Closed Monday

Tesoro Ristorante has been Long Island's pride and joy for the past 23 years. Through years of expansions and redecorating, Tesoro has remained elegant but simple and comfortable. Tesoro's menu encompasses many regions of Italy from North to South, specializing in daily fresh pasta, imported fresh fish, and their most tender veal.

Tesoro can also accommodate private family or corporate functions from 30 - 120 persons. Antonio or Angelo will personally tailor your menu.

eggplant napoleon

Serves: 4 appetizers

2 large eggplants, sliced lengthwise

2 roasted red bell peppers, peeled, seeded and diced

1 large Maui onion, diced fine

1 8-ounce can of black olives, chopped fine

8 ounces thinly sliced smoked mozzarella cheese

1 pound thinly sliced grilled mushrooms

2 ounces premium olive oil

4 cloves crushed garlic

1 ounce dry or fresh assorted herbs chopped very fine

Tomato-Balsamic Vinaigrette

1 cup peeled, seeded and diced tomatoes

½ cup finely chopped white onion

¼ cup chopped basil

⅓ cup Dijon mustard

⅓ cup balsamic vinegar

1 ½ cups olive oil

2 tablespoons sugar

1 teaspoon pepper

1 teaspoon salt

1 teaspoon Worcestershire Sauce

Lightly brush eggplant with olive oil, garlic and herbs. Grill on medium heat, browning on both sides. Set aside to cool. Layer all ingredients as follows: eggplant, cheese, chopped olives, diced onions, diced roasted bell peppers and mushrooms into two layers and finish with the eggplant.

Cut loaf into two inch widths and place on a bed of tomato-balsamic vinaigrette. Garnish with julienne of basil and grated Romano cheese.

Tomato-Balsamic Vinaigrette

Mix all ingredients together in a large bowl, excluding oil. Let ingredients sit for 10 minutes. Then slowly add oil while whisking so the ingredients do not separate. If the dressing is too thick add cool water to thin it out slightly. Chill before using.

Bon Appetite.

Enjoy this appetizer with a bottle of light red wine such as Castelllo di Borghese Pinot Noir or San Giovese. Our San Giovese vines were planted this year, so look for our first bottling in 2007!

VOILA!
The Bistro

244 Lake Avenue
St. James

Phone: 631-584-5686

www.voilathebistro.com

HAMID MENDOUNE, CHEF AND OWNER

VISA, MasterCard, American Express

HOURS:

Lunch
Monday - Saturday
Noon - 2:00 pm

Dinner
Monday - Saturday
5:00 pm - 11:00 pm
Closed Sundays

If you are looking for a French bistro, Voila! does not disappoint. Attentive service, quiet atmosphere and attractive ambience add to the charm of this New York Times rated "very good" restaurant.

sashimi of salmon

Serves: 14

4 pounds Norwegian salmon (1/2 whole salmon)
3 cups kosher salt
1/2 cup chopped cilantro
1/2 cup chopped fresh ginger

1/2 cup mixed herbs (thyme, oregano, lavender)
1/3 cup crushed pepper
1/3 cup red chili pepper
1/3 cup granulated sugar

4 tablespoons soy sauce
9 tablespoons cold water
6 teaspoons molasses
2 teaspoons lemon juice

Mix together all dry ingredients and pour over salmon with skin side down. Refrigerate overnight. Next day, remove the dry ingredients by cleaning the salmon with cold water.

Combine liquid ingredients, pour over fish, flesh side up and refrigerate for at least 8 hours. Remove fish from liquid. Thicken liquid ingredients by cooking on medium heat until it is reduced half way. Be careful that it's not too salty. If it is salty, add more water. Cool.

Slice salmon very fine and serve it with micro green salad. Pour dressing lightly over fish and salad.

I love this type of recipe because you can serve white or red wine. To enhance the tasting experience at wine dinners, I will pair two wines with one course. Try Castello di Borghese Barrel Fermented Chardonnay or Castello di Borghese Pinot Noir. You decide.

GREAT TASTES
OF LONG ISLAND

SOUPS & SALADS

soups & salads

The 1770 House Restaurant & Inn

143 MAIN STREET · EAST HAMPTON

Tel: 631-324-1770 · Fax: 631-324-3504

www.1770house.com

KEVIN PENNER, CHEF

Reservations Required

Open Daily 6:00 pm -10:00 pm

All Credit Cards Accepted

Casual Neat Attire

The ever-changing menu at this historic inn offers wondrous appetizers, splendid entrees as well as unforgettable desserts. The tavern, while maintaining the charm of its era, is hauntingly romantic. You will be very welcome in this house.

chilled maine lobster salad with asparagus in 25 year old balsamic vinegar

Serves: 4

For the Lobster
3 one pound Maine
  lobsters, very much
  alive
1 large carrot, chopped
1 onion, chopped
1 bunch celery,
  chopped
1 tablespoon black
  peppercorns

3 bay leaves
2 gallons water

For the Salad
One bunch of
  asparagus, blanched
  and chopped into
  ¾ inch pieces
2 cups crème fraiche

1 cup mayonnaise
Zest from 3 lemons
1 tablespoon chopped
  tarragon
1 tablespoon chopped
  chives
1 cup mesclun greens
Reserved lobster meat
25 year old balsamic
  vinegar

For the Lobster
Place the carrot, celery, onion, peppercorns and bay leaves in a pot and pour in the
water. Bring to a boil over high heat. Plunge lobsters into the water and cook until
completely done, about 7 minutes. Remove the lobsters and shock in a large bowl of
ice water until cooled, about 10 minutes. Remove the tail and claw meat from the
lobsters, coarsely chop and refrigerate until needed.

For the Salad
Stir together the crème fraiche, mayonnaise, lemon zest, tarragon and chives. Season
to taste with salt and pepper. In a separate bowl, combine lobster and asparagus.
Add enough of the crème fraiche dressing to liberally coat them. Place a small bed of
mesclun greens on each plate, mound lobster salad on top and drizzle with
balsamic vinegar.

*Our stainless steel Sauvignon Blanc makes its mark with the gorgeous layers of
herbal flavors and textures in this tantalizing dish.*

430-16 North Country Road
St. James

---- New Italian American Cuisine ----

Anthony Cambria, Owner/Chef

Phone: 631-862-8060

www.bellavitacitygrill.com

Online Reservations Recommended

Attire: Casual Neat

VISA, MasterCard, American Express, Discover Card

Hours:
Monday - Thursday 11:30 am - 10:00 pm
Friday 11:30 am - 11:00 pm
Saturday 4:00 pm - 11:00 pm
Sunday 4:00 pm - 9:00 pm

Opened in December of 1996, this family operated and chef-owned restaurant in St. James is an intimate affair serving creative Italian-American cuisine. Bella Vita City Grill is committed to providing a pleasant atmosphere, incorporating an innovative menu with friendly service. They offer an extensive variety of tasty and tongue tantalizing treats. From robust dinners to exquisite desserts, Bella Vita City Grill provides patrons with a taste and flavor to please any palate!

bella vita city grill's famous house chopped salad

Serves: 1-2

For Salad
8 ounces field green salad chopped into 1 inch pieces
4 ounces red peppers/ roasted on the grill, peeled and cut into ¼ inch strips

4 ounces canned artichoke hearts/grill whole then cut in quarters
4 ounces sundried tomatoes, cut in strips
2 ounces sliced black olives
1 ounce pine nuts/oven roasted

For Balsamic Dressing
2 ounces balsamic vinegar
6 ounces soy oil
1 garlic clove, minced
¼ cup sugar
Salt and pepper to taste

For Salad
Combine field green salad, red peppers, artichoke hearts, sundried tomatoes, black olives and pine nuts.

For Balsamic Dressing
Combine balsamic vinegar, soy oil, minced garlic clove, sugar, salt and pepper.

Add dressing to salad, toss and serve.

Excellent with Castello di Borghese Pinot Blanc.

Butterfields

661 Old Willets Path
Hauppauge

New American Cuisine

Phone: 631-851-1507

www.butterfieldsrestaurant.biz

JERRY SUPPA, CHEF/OWNER

Reservations Recommended

ATTIRE: Casual Neat

HOURS:
Monday - Friday: Noon - 10:00 pm
Saturday: 5:00 pm - 11:00 pm
<u>Happy Hour</u>
Monday - Friday: 4:00 pm - 7:00 pm
free bar food & drink specials

Visa, MasterCard, American Express accepted

Tucked away in an industrial park, this New American restaurant located in Hauppauge has "hit the ground running" and is "worth the trip" with Chef Jerry Suppa's "innovative presentations" and "wonderful" dishes; the "impeccable service", "pretty" decor (some tables have loveseats) makes for a "fine experience."
Zagat Survey 2004/2005

watercress endive salad with bleu cheese, pink grapefruit, garlic chips & champagne vinaigrette

Serves: 6

Salad
2 bunches watercress (top leaves cut and washed)
3 pieces Belgium endive (halved, cored, then julienned)
2 heads California frisee (washed)
6 heads baby red oak leaf lettuce (washed)
2 pink grapefruits (segmented)

1 cup Maytag bleu cheese (crumbled)

Garlic Chips
15 cloves garlic, peeled
Cold milk
2 quarts canola oil

Vinaigrette
1/2 cup seasoned rice wine vinegar
1/2 cup Champagne vinegar

1 teaspoon Dijon mustard
2 cups pink grapefruit juice
Juice of 1 lime
1 tablespoon Mirin (Asian rice wine)
1/2 cup extra virgin olive oil
1 1/2 cups canola oil
Salt and pepper

For the Salad
Pre-wash the watercress, frisee, and red oak leaf. Gently spin salad in salad spinner to dry leaves. Mix in Belgium endive and reserve salad in refrigerator.

For the Garlic Chips
Thinly slice garlic cloves on a mandoline or as thin as possible with a sharp paring knife. Put garlic slices in a sauté pan with enough cold milk to cover and bring to a boil. Strain garlic and repeat this process 3 times (blanching the garlic in milk removes the bitterness and brings out the sweetness in the garlic). Pat the garlic dry. Fill a 4 quart sauce pot halfway with canola oil at 300°F and fry garlic until lightly golden brown. Remove from oil and rest on paper towels. Season with salt.

For the Vinaigrette
In a blender, mix vinegars, mustard, grapefruit juice, lime juice and Mirin. Emulsify with oils and season with salt and pepper.

Assembly
Dress salad with just enough of the viniagrette to coat the lettuce. Toss in the crumbled bleu cheese and half the grapefruit segments and season with salt and pepper. Place the salad in the center of each plate with the remaining grapefruit segments on the side. Sprinkle the salad with garlic chips and serve. Then enjoy!!!

This bright innovative salad is a lavish treat with Castello di Borghese Riesling.

Celebrating our 10th Anniversary!

Cafe Joelle
on Main Street

25 MAIN STREET
SAYVILLE, NY 11782

Phone: 631-589-4600
Fax: 631-589-4632

Casual Eclectic American Cuisine

STEVE SANDS AND JULES BUITRON, OWNERS
LENNY POLMARI, EXECUTIVE CHEF

Casual neat attire

HOURS
Lunch:
Monday - Saturday 11:00 am - 4:00 pm
Sunday Brunch 11:00 am - 3:00 pm
Dinner:
Monday - Thursday 4:00 pm - 10:00 pm
Friday - Saturday 4:00 pm - 11:00 pm
Sunday - 3:00 pm - 9:00 pm

Pasta nights: Monday and Tuesday

Credit cards: amex, visa, mc, diners club

As quaint as the town of Sayville where it's situated, this is a popular, casual European style bistro which features pasta, veal, chicken, lamb, seafood, the freshest fish available and innovative daily specials. This popular lunch spot, offering a variety of salads, sandwiches, and burgers, is most famous for their creative soups.

Zagat guide boasts "every town should have a restaurant like this".

soups & salads 48

grilled chicken with apple and brie salad with cranberry vinaigrette

Serves: 2 entrees or 4-6 side dishes

6 8-ounce chicken breasts, grilled or broiled
6 8-ounce assorted salad greens, cut and washed
1 granny smith apple, cored and sliced
6 ounces Brie cheese, sliced

2 plum tomatoes, cut in quarters
½ small red onion, thinly sliced
2 tablespoons canned whole cranberries

4 ounces Italian vinaigrette, bottled or homemade
Salt and pepper to taste

Grill or broil chicken breasts seasoned with salt and pepper. Cook fully.

In a large mixing bowl, add salad greens, apples, plum tomatoes and red onions. In a small bowl, mix cranberries and vinaigrette dressing. Mix together well. Pour over salad and gently toss together. Arrange salad on serving bowl or platter. Top with sliced, cooked chicken and sliced Brie.

Chef's Note: A very refreshing light salad.

A beautiful luncheon recipe to be paired with a Castello di Borghese Pinot Blanc. This would be an easy picnic centerpiece for the boat or beach.

Courtyard Café

3505 Veterans Memorial Highway
Ronkonkoma
631-467-4848

NEW AMERICAN CUISINE

www.thecourtyardcafe.com

JOAN CAELIN, OWNER
JACK NUMA, CHEF

All major credit cards accepted

Hours
Lunch
Monday - Friday
11:30 am - 3:00 pm

Dinner
Monday - Saturday
5:00 pm - 10:00 pm
Sunday
4:00 pm - 9:00 pm

Reservations Recommended

ATTIRE: Dressy Casual

A beautiful flowered walkway leads guests to a delightful dining experience at the Courtyard Café. With a warm greeting at the door, cheerful wait staff, snowy white linens, seasonal floral arrangements, and soothing background music, the perfect relaxing atmosphere welcomes you. The lunch, early bird, and dinner menus are diverse, featuring a variety of flavors to appeal to the senses. Cast away your stress and satisfy your taste buds in style at this charming restaurant.

soups & salads 50

warm pears & gorgonzola salad

Serves: 6

Salad
2 endive cut into rings
1 head radicchio, torn into
    pieces
1 bunch frisee
2 tablespoons chopped
    flat parsley
½ cup walnut halves

8 ounces crumbled
    gorgonzola
2 D'Anjou pears halved,
    sliced, cored and cut
    lengthwise
Salt and pepper
2 tablespoons butter
½ tablespoon sugar

Walnut Vinaigrette
3 tablespoons red wine
    vinegar
2 tablespoons Dijon
    mustard
¾ cup walnut oil
Salt and pepper

Walnut Vinaigrette
Combine vinegar and mustard. Gradually whisk in walnut oil to emulsify.
Season with salt and pepper.

For Salad
Combine endive, radicchio, frisee, parsley and walnuts. Dress salad with walnut
vinaigrette. Top with crumbled gorgonzola. Sauté pear slices in butter and sugar
until caramelized. Place warm pears onto salad.

Chef's Note: Walnut Vinaigrette can be made ahead of time.

 Castello di Borghese Merlot or Merlot Reserve, opulent with vibrant freshness,
pair equally depending where this course comes in the dinner.

HEMINGWAY'S
AMERICAN BAR AND GRILL

1885 Wantagh Avenue, Wantagh
Phone: 516-781-2700
Fax: 516-781-2781

www.hemingwaysgrill.com

ROBERT SULLIVAN, OWNER
GEORGE CANGIONO, CHEF

Open 7 Days a week
Monday - Saturday 11:30 am - 11:00 pm
Sunday - 10:30 am - 10:00 pm

Credit Cards Accepted: Visa, MC, AmEx, and Diner's

"Great atmosphere! The food is excellent, the service is excellent, and the drinks are fantastic !!!"

"Hemingway's Bar and Grill's generous servings of creative American food make this warm friendly Wantagh grill a magnet, especially for those who appreciate a lively bar scene." ~ Zagat Restaurant Guide

goat cheese salad with sundried cranberries, brandied pecans and crumbled goat cheese

Serves: 1

2 ½ ounces of
    mesclun greens
1 ounce of sundried
    cranberries
1 ½ ounces of
    brandied pecans

3 ½ ounces of goat
    cheese
1 vine ripened tomato,
    sliced
3 slices cucumber
2 ounces lite raspberry
    vinaigrette

For the Brandied Pecans
Sauté pecans in 1 tablespoon of butter, 1 ounce of brandy, and 1 tablespoon of brown sugar. Place on a sheet tray in oven at 350°F for 5 minutes to dry (let cool before adding to salad). The pecans can be prepared ahead of time.

For the Salad
Toss mesclun greens with lite raspberry vinaigrette, place in center of plate. Add 3 tomato slices and 3 cucumber slices around salad, top salad with pecans, cranberries and goat cheese. Sprinkle black pepper around plate rim.

Chef's Note: The goat cheese blends well with the vinaigrette. Brandied pecans and sundried cranberries add texture. Good with chicken, fish and shrimp.

 Invite a friend, double the recipe and open a bottle of Castello di Borghese Sauvignon Blanc or Riesling.

Panama Hatties

872 East Jericho Turnpike
Huntington Station

- AMERICAN CUISINE -

Phone: 631-351-1727

www.panamahatties.com

MATTHEW HISSIGER, OWNER/EXECUTIVE CHEF
KENT MONKAN, CHEF DE CUISINE

Reservations Recommended

ATTIRE: Upscale Casual

VISA, MasterCard, American Express, Diner's Club, Discover

HOURS:
Lunch Monday - Friday / Noon - 3:00 pm
Dinner Monday-Friday / 5:30 pm - 9:30 pm
Saturday 5:00 pm - 10:30 pm / Sunday 4:00 pm - 9:00 pm

Nestled inconspicuously in an unassuming strip mall, the elegant atmosphere that awaits diners at Panama Hatties will delight even the most jaded restaurant critic. Contemporary American cuisine is artfully presented in an unpretentious manner. Gracious service will go unnoticed as waiters glide through the dining room. Rated four stars from Newsday and The New York Times, Panama Hatties continues to sizzle with excitement.

sherried lobster bisque

Serves: 8

4 1½ -pound lobsters
1 medium onion
    (medium dice)
1 carrot (medium
    dice)
3 cloves garlic
    (smashed)

3 bay leaves
1 teaspoon fennel seed
4 ounces butter for roux
4 ounces flour for roux
4 tomatoes (roughly
    chopped)
5 sprigs thyme

2 cups sherry
3 tablespoons olive oil
½ cup heavy cream
Salt and pepper to taste

For Roux
Melt butter in a small sauce pan. Add flour, stirring on low heat. Cook for approximately 5 minutes until a nutty aroma is present. Reserve on side.

Poaching Lobster
Bring a large pot of water to a boil. Add in lobsters and cook for 6 minutes.
Remove from pot and place in an ice water bath to stop the cooking process.
Pull all of the meat from the shells and reserve. Clean the shells in water and reserve.

Soup
In a 5 quart sauce pot, heat olive oil. Add onion, carrot and garlic stirring constantly for five minutes. Add in lobster shells, keeping the heat on high for five minutes.
Add fennel seed, bay leaves, and tomatoes. Keep stirring for five minutes.
Add one cup of sherry and thyme sprigs. Add in cold water just to cover ingredients.
Bring to a simmer and cook for one hour. Keep at a simmer, do not boil.
Strain broth after an hour. Pour back into a clean pot and bring to a simmer.
Gradually add in roux, whisking constantly.

Season with salt and pepper to taste. Slowly add in heavy cream, followed by remaining 1 cup sherry. Strain through a fine mesh sieve and serve with reserved lobster meat.

Sumptuous ingredients are a perfect match for Castello di Borghese Barrel Fermented Chardonnay and Chef Monkan proves it.

Tex-Mex Cuisine

10 Grace Avenue
Great Neck
Tel: 516-829-5305 / Fax: 516-829-4167
www.panchosbordergrill.com

JEFF MOSS, DAVE NEYMAN, GARY STEINER, AND DARREN LORA, OWNERS
JULIO GONZALEZ, CHEF

Visa, AmEx, Mastercard, and Discover Accepted

LUNCH: Monday - Friday 11:30 am - 4:00 pm
DINNER: Monday - Thursday 4:00 pm - 10:00 pm
Friday and Saturday 4:00 pm - 11:00 pm
Sunday 4:00 pm - 9:00 pm

Pancho's Border Grill has brought the finest in fresh Tex-Mex cuisine to Long Island's North Shore since 1991. Pancho's features a wide array of authentic Tex-Mex specialties including sizzling fajitas, frozen margaritas, homemade guacamole, tender baby back ribs and create-your-own combination platters. They also offer a full service bar featuring an extensive collection of designer tequilas, as well as a full selection of steaks, salads, seafood, and the best avocado cheeseburger you've ever tasted! For younger clientele, Pancho's offers kids' meals guaranteed to please even the pickiest palates.

Corporate catering is available for any occasion, at any location. Regardless of whether you need to feed 20 or 220, Pancho's can deliver fresh, hot, and delicious food to your home or office.

black bean soup

Serves: 6

16 ounces (about 2½ cups) dry black beans, cleaned

3 strips bacon, diced

1 medium Spanish onion, peeled and finely chopped

1 medium green bell pepper, stemmed, seeded and diced

3 garlic cloves, chopped

1 teaspoon dried oregano

1 teaspoon cumin

2 bay leaves

½ cup cilantro, chopped

½ cup red wine

2½ quarts water or chicken stock

½ cup crumbled Mexican queso fresco or pressed, salted farmer's cheese (optional)

Salt and pepper to taste

Soak the beans overnight in cold water. Render the bacon in a 5 quart pot over medium-high heat until it is browned. Add onion, green bell pepper, garlic, cumin and oregano. Lower the heat and cook, stirring frequently, until the vegetables wilt and onions become translucent. Add red wine, bay leaves and cilantro. Raise heat to medium-high, bring to a boil and cook for 5 minutes. Add water or stock. Drain the beans and add them to pot. Cover and simmer until beans are tender, about 1 hour. If you see beans peeking up through liquid, add hot water to cover them by ½ inch. Remove half the mixture and purée in food processor. Return to pot and stir well. Taste and season with salt and pepper. Ladle soup into bowls and garnish with cheese.

For the true nuances of North Fork wine country try Castello di Borghese Merlot.

GREAT TASTES
OF LONG ISLAND

PASTA & RICE DISHES

pasta & rice dishes

EAST HAMPTON POINT

295 Three Mile Harbor Road
East Hampton

Tel: (631) 329-2800 / Fax: (631) 329-2876

www.easthamptonpoint.com

Matthew Ross, Chef

Casual Attire

Open Weekends Only:
April 1st - Memorial Day

Memorial Day - Labor Day:
Lunch
Noon - 3:00 pm daily
Dinner
5:00 pm - 10:00 pm weekdays
5:00 pm - 11:00 pm weekends

Credit Cards: Visa, Mastercard, Amex

Chef Matthew Ross serves "New American Contemporary Cuisine" with an emphasis on fresh local produce, seafood and poultry. The wine list is carefully chosen to complement all aspects of the menu and wines are selected from all over the world.

lobster risotto

Serves: 4

Lobster Stock
2 tablespoons olive oil
1 large onion diced
2 celery stalks, diced
2 carrots, diced
2 leeks, diced (wash well)
6 garlic cloves
8 cups water
1 cup white wine
1/4 cup tomato paste
1 generous bunch of thyme
3 bay leaves
2 2-pound lobsters

Risotto
1/4 cup olive oil
1 small white onion, diced
2 cups Aborio rice
2 cups white wine
5 cups warm lobster stock
3 tablespoons butter
1/2 cup Parmesan cheese, grated
1/2 cup Asiago cheese, grated
1 tablespoon fresh parsley, chopped

Sauce
4 ounces chanterelle mushrooms
1 bunch asparagus, trimmed for the tips
1/2 cup lobster stock
2 tablespoons butter
Lobster meat
1 tablespoon fresh thyme, chopped

Lobster Stock
Sweat vegetables in oil until tender. Add tomato paste. Cook for 5 minutes on medium heat. Add white wine and water. Bring to a simmer. Add herbs and put live lobsters in broth for 12 minutes. Clean meat from lobster and reserve. Add shells back to stock and cook for twenty minutes. Strain and keep warm.

Risotto (rice must be stirred constantly throughout the process to prevent sticking)
Sweat onions in oil until soft. Add rice and cook for 2 minutes. Add white wine, reduce heat to medium low (stirring). Cook until wine is absorbed. Add enough lobster stock to cover the rice (second time, stirring constantly) until al dente (you may have to repeat a third time - it's important to taste rice often). Remove from heat and add the 3 tablespoons of butter, Parmesan cheese, Asiago cheese and parsley. Adjust the seasoning. Stir until creamy. Risotto takes about 15-20 minutes to make.

Sauce
Sauté mushrooms in 1 tablespoon butter until golden brown. Add asparagus tips and shallots. Add 1/2 cup of lobster stock. Bring to a simmer. Add lobster meat, 1 tablespoon butter and thyme.

To Serve
Spoon risotto onto 4 plates. Place 1/2 tail and one claw on top. Place vegetables and sauce around the risotto.

Chef's Note: The amount of lobster stock you need to make the risotto is approximate. You may need to use less or more. The important thing is to use enough to cover the rice.

Without a doubt Castello di Borghese Barrel Fermented Chardonnay. This combination is a family favorite.

GALLERIA DOMINICK RESTAURANT

Northern Italian Cuisine

238 Post Avenue, Westbury
516-997-7373

DOMINICK ZELKO, OWNER
PABLO ARTURO ROMERO, CHEF

Lunch
Monday - Friday Noon - 3:00 pm

Dinner
Monday - Thursday 5:00 pm - 10:00 pm
Friday - Saturday 5:00 pm - 11:00 pm
Sunday 2:00 pm - 9:00 pm

Credit Cards: AmEx, Visa, MC

Galleria Dominick is an authentic Northern Italian restaurant that offers exceptional food and service in an elegant atmosphere.

pasta veal ragu

Serves: 4

1 pound of veal, cut into cubes
1 large onion, diced
2 small shallots, diced

2 tablespoons tomato paste
12 ounce can of chopped tomatoes

3 tablespoons olive oil
1 cup of chicken stock
Wondra gravy thickener

In a large saucepan, sauté onions, and shallots with oil until golden brown. Add veal and simmer until all water has evaporated and the veal begins to turn brown in color. Add tomatoes and tomato paste, stir for about 5 minutes. Add chicken stock, lower heat and cover pan. Let it simmer for at least 45 minutes or until meat is tender. Add more chicken stock if desired. Sprinkle with Wondra gravy thickener and stir in until sauce thickens. Serve over pasta of your choice.

 Castello di Borghese Merlot Reserve is an excellent choice.

15 Wall Street, Huntington
Tel: 631-549-0055 / Fax: 631-549-3545
jonathansristorante.com

Italian Cuisine

Open 7 Days
Lunch
11:30 am to 2:30 pm Monday - Saturday
Dinner
5:00 pm to 10:00 pm Monday - Thursday
5:00 pm to 10:30 pm Friday and Saturday
4:00 pm to 9:00 pm Sunday

ROBERTO ORNATO - OWNER
TITO ONOFRE - CHEF

Prix Fixe: Sunday, Monday - Thursday all night
Reservations: Suggested
Credit Cards: Amex, Visa, MC, Diners Club
Attire: Jackets not required
Accessibility: Handicapped accessible

The setting of this Huntington landmark is delightful with an atmosphere that combines European flavor with a casual country look, contemporary Italian menu, and a courteous and knowledgeable staff. Jonathan's was recognized with a Zagat 2001 "Award of Distinction".

mushroom risotto

Serves: 4 to 6

½ to ¾ pound fresh
  porcini mushrooms
8 cups chicken stock
½ stick unsalted
  butter

1 medium-size yellow
  onion, finely chopped
2 ½ cups Arborio or
  Carnaroli rice
  (Italian long-grain)
Salt

To Finish the Risotto
4 ounces Parmigiano-
  Reggiano cheese
Drizzle of truffle oil

Remove the porcini stems and add them to the stock. Slice the caps crosswise about ¼ inch thick. In a medium size sauté pan over medium-low heat, melt 2 tablespoons of the butter. Add the mushroom slices and cook, stirring frequently until soft (about five minutes). Set aside. Bring the stock to a boil and immediately reduce to a simmer.

In a large sauté pan over medium heat, melt the remaining 2 tablespoons butter. Add the onion and cook, stirring, until translucent. Raise the heat, add the rice and stir vigorously until the grains are translucent and the "pearl" in each grain appears clearly. Immediately reduce the heat to low and add two or three ladles' worth of simmering stock, just barely enough to cover the rice. Season with salt. Stir briefly. When air holes start to appear in surface, add another ladleful of stock. Continue to cook and add stock, tasting for salt from time to time.

When the risotto is about two ladles' worth of stock from being fully cooked, stir in the mushroom slices and continue cooking. When fully cooked, remove from the heat. To finish the risotto, add the grated Parmigiano, stirring again. Place on hot serving plates, add a drizzle of truffle oil and serve immediately.

Chef's Note: Any fresh mushroom works with risotto. Fresh shiitake or Portobello mushrooms are ideal. Or if you like, just mix all of them and have fun!

 Redolent of cherry, a Castello di Borghese Pinot Noir is an earthy match.

La Parmigiana

44-48 Hampton Road, Southampton
Tel: (631) 283-8030 / Fax: (631) 283-8065
www.laparmigiana.com

Celestino Gambino, Owner
Joanne Manglaviti, Chef

CASUAL ATTIRE

All major credit cards accepted

Monday - Saturday 11:30 am to 10:30 pm
Sunday 12:30 pm to 10:00 pm

"Fantastic, old-style Southern Italian cooking" ~ Zagats 2002

Main dishes, like fettuccini or eggplant parmesan, are big enough to share with an entire family and keep people coming back for more.

penne ala vodka

Serves: 4

1 tablespoon butter
1 tablespoon mascarpone
1 cup heavy cream
½ cup vodka

2 tablespoons tomato
  sauce
4 leaves of fresh basil

2 tablespoons Romano
cheese
1 pound penne

First put the butter in a frying pan and let it melt. Then put in the vodka and let it evaporate. When the flame goes down, put in the heavy cream, tomato sauce, mascarpone and basil. Let it cook on low for 15 minutes until it gets creamy. Cook the pasta, drain it and put it in with the cream sauce. Add cheese and serve.

Chef's Note: You can make it ahead of time and freeze it.

 Castello di Borghese Cabernet Franc is perky with a lively mouth-feel. The combination of this creamy, rich pasta and Cabernet Franc is festive and satisfying.

PASTA
....
PASTA

234 East Main Street, Port Jefferson
www.pastapasta.net
(631) 331-5335

Creative Italian/ American Cuisine

Executive Chef - Jason Kuebler
Casual neat attire

Lunch:
Monday - Saturday 11:30 am - 3:00 pm
Dinner:
Monday - Thursday 4:30 pm - 10:00 pm
Friday and Saturday 4:30 pm - 11:00 pm
Sunday (dinner only) 3:00 pm - 9:00 pm

Credit cards: amex, visa, mc, diners club

Reservations recommended

Situated in the historic waterfront town of Port Jefferson, Pasta Pasta has become one of the premier restaurants on the North Shore. More than just pasta, it offers a diverse menu featuring veal, chicken, steak, the freshest fish available and of course our innovative pastas and pizzas. Decorated in the casual and comfortable style of a Tuscan Villa, the dining rooms boast light wood accents, vases filled with fresh flowers, candlelit tables, antique mirrors, framed art prints and gracefully draped curtains.

rigatoni with shrimp, spinach & goat cheese

Serves: 2 main or 6-8 side dishes

16 ounces cooked rigatoni
½ - ¾ pound medium shrimp cleaned and deveined
2 cups heavy cream
1 cup marinara sauce, homemade or jarred

1 ounce fresh spinach, cleaned
2 tablespoons fresh basil, cleaned and chopped
1 teaspoon garlic, chopped

4 ounces goat cheese, sliced into rounds
2 tablespoons butter
Salt and pepper to taste

Add butter to a warm sauté pan. Add garlic and sauté for 1 minute. Add shrimp and sauté for 3 minutes. Add cream, marinara sauce, fresh basil, spinach, salt and pepper to taste. Bring to a boil. Reduce sauce by ¼. Toss in warm cooked rigatoni.

Adjust seasoning (if you need more sauce, add more cream). Pour or spoon into serving bowls. Top with goat cheese.

Chef's Note: A very hearty pasta dish. One of our customers' favorites.

Castello di Borghese Estate Chardonnay is clean, crisp and elegant. Hints of vanilla create a gracious well-balanced dinner wine.

Tuscan House

673 Osborne Avenue, Riverhead
Tel: (631) 727-2330 / Fax: (631) 727-2342

Northern Italian Cuisine

William Oster, Chef/Co-Owner

Attire: Casual but proper

VISA, MasterCard, American Express

Hours:
Monday - Saturday
Lunch - 11:30 am - 3:30 pm
Dinner - 3:30 pm - 10:00 pm
Sunday
3:00 pm - 10:00 pm

Situated a little off the beaten path, this restaurant is sure to please. The recipes are authentic and well presented. For pasta lovers, there are a wide range of dishes to choose from, all with light and flavorful sauces. Don't forget to order dessert…you won't be disappointed.

spaghetti o vermicelli con le vongole in bianco (spaghetti or vermicelli in clam sauce)

Serves: 4 to 6

1½ pounds small clams, such as Manila clams, cockles, or littlenecks, in the shell
Coarse-grained salt
1 lemon, cut in half
¾ cup extra-virgin olive oil

3 large cloves garlic, peeled and finely chopped
1 pound dried vermicelli or spaghetti, preferably imported Italian
Salt and abundant freshly ground black pepper

20 large sprigs Italian parsley, leaves only, coarsely chopped

To Serve
10 sprigs Italian parsley, leaves only

Rinse the clams several times under cold running water. Soak the clams for 30 minutes in a bowl of cold water containing 1 tablespoon coarse salt and the squeezed lemon halves. Drain and rinse the clams again under cold running water.

Place a stockpot of cold water over medium heat to cook the pasta, and place a large skillet containing the oil and garlic over medium heat.

When the oil is warm and barely starts sautéing the garlic, raise the heat to high, add the clams and cover. Cook for 2 minutes, shaking the skillet several times. By this time, the water for the pasta should be boiling. Add coarse salt to taste, then add the pasta and cook for 8-11 minutes, depending on the brand (1 minute less than for normal al dente).

Season the clams well with salt and pepper and add the parsley. By this time, all the clams should be open (discard any that are still closed). Cover the skillet and cook for 4 minutes more, mixing frequently. Drain the pasta, add it to the skillet, and mix very well to coat the pasta with the juices.

Transfer the contents of the skillet to a large serving platter, sprinkle with the parsley, and serve hot, with the clams still in their shells.

Variation: Even though this is a "white" sauce, some people add 3-4 whole cherry tomatoes.

Chef's Note: I know it is very difficult to convince restaurateurs, but adding even a drop of heavy cream completely destroys this dish. The combination of the oil and the juices coming out from the clams as they open and cook forms a wonderful emulsion that is the only sauce you need to toss with the pasta.

This is one of the Borghese family's favorite recipes. It is beautiful with Castello di Borghese Sauvignon Blanc. This 100% stainless steel line is a classic. There just isn't a better pairing.

Vittorio's
wine bar and restaurant

184 Broadway, Amityville
Tel: (631) 264-3333 / Fax: (631) 598-7166

Michael Esposito, Owner
John Ringle, Chef

ITALIAN CONTINENTAL CUISINE

Open 7 days a week
Lunch: Monday - Friday Noon - 3 pm
Dinner: Until 10 pm weekdays, 11 pm weekends
Reservations Recommended on weekends

All major credit cards accepted

The chef of this Italian Continental style restaurant handpicks all the ingredients himself, assuring the very freshest quality foods. Some customer favorites are Chilean sea bass, New York strip steak, and the open cannoli dessert. For steak lovers there is a traditional steakhouse menu every Wednesday. The bar area features a wide range of drinks including over 40 different martinis, a selection of 110 bottles of wine and 85 varieties by the glass. On and off premises catering is available for all occasions.

penne's from heaven

Serves: 2

3 ounces extra virgin olive
   oil
6-8 garlic cloves
1/2 pound penne pasta
   (cook to package
   directions)
10 broccoli spears
2 plum tomatoes diced
   in 1/2 inch cubes

12 ounces chicken breast,
   cut in 1/2 inch strips
1 sprig rosemary
2 ounces sun-dried
   tomatoes
8 ounces chicken stock
Salt and pepper to taste

Sauté garlic in olive oil until golden brown.

Add strips of chicken breast, sauté for 2 minutes, stirring constantly.

Add rest of ingredients together. Cook for 3-4 minutes.

Add cooked pasta and fold together.

Castello di Borghese Cabernet Franc blends brilliantly with this heavenly pasta.

ENTRÉES

entrées

75 MAIN

75 Main Street
Southampton

Phone: 631-283-7575

www.75main.com

Noah Jaques, Executive Chef

Reservations Recommended

HOURS:
Breakfast/Brunch
9:00 am - 4:00 pm
Dinner
Monday-Thursday, Sunday
5:00 pm - 9:00 pm
Friday and Saturday
5:00 pm - 10:00 pm

Bar
Open until 4:00 am

The New York Times rated 75 Main one of the "Top Ten Hamptons Restaurants". This seasoned veteran of the Southampton social scene offers something for everyone, from its convenient location and versatile Italian-Amalfi Coast décor to its outstanding dining selections. If a versatile, fun, relaxed atmosphere sounds appealing, head over to 75 Main.

pan seared sea bass w/vegetable mousaka & tatziki relish

Serves: 4

4 6-ounce portions of cleaned sea bass, salt and peppered

1 large eggplant, sliced ¼ inch thick

1 bag baby spinach

1 bunch asparagus, trimmed

4 16-ounce cans roasted red peppers

1 log of goat cheese

1½ cups of half and half

Tatziki Relish

1 seedless cucumber, diced

8 ounces plain yogurt

1 teaspoon salt

¼ teaspoon pepper

1 teaspoon sugar

Lemon juice of ½ lemon

¼ of small red onion, diced

Preheat oven to 425°F. In a 4 inch baking dish follow this step twice for 2 layers: eggplant, asparagus, spinach, roasted red peppers, and goat cheese spread. Goat cheese spread is made by combining half and half to goat cheese log and whipping until creamy. Bake with foil cover 45 minutes to l hour. Heat a sauté pan with oil until it starts to smoke. Salt and pepper sea bass on both sides and sear skin side up until golden brown and crispy. Finish fish in oven with mousaka (about 12 to 15 minutes).

Tatziki Relish

Dice cucumber medium dice. Add yogurt to bowl with cucumbers. Combine salt, sugar, lemon juice, pepper and 1 tablespoon finely diced red onion. Combine all ingredients and chill for at least an hour. Use relish as sauce for fish. Cut mousaka into squares for serving.

Tatziki Relish is better if made a day in advance.

Castello di Borghese Barrel Fermented Chardonnay will highlight the subtle elements of this dish.

Abel Conklin's
Fine Food & Wines

54 New Street, Huntington
Tel: 631-385-1919 / Fax: 631-385-1955

www.abelconklins.com

<u>Lunch</u>
Monday - Friday 11:30 am - 3:30 pm

<u>Dinner</u>
Sunday - Thursday 4:30 pm- 10:00 pm
Friday - Saturday 4:30 pm - 11:00 pm

JULIO LEON, CHEF

Beautiful oak paneling with mahogany accents is the elegant setting of this warm and inviting restaurant, established in 1986 in the historic house built in 1841 by Abel Conklin.

This eclectic steakhouse serves Prime Aged Steaks and fresh seafood daily. Specialties include live Maine lobsters, veal, lamb, and pork chops. The juicy porterhouse prime aged steak is mouth-watering and the aging and butchering are done in house. Not only is the restaurant a traditional steakhouse, but it also offers other cuisines.

lomo saltado
(jumping beef sauté)

Serves: 5-6

32-ounce beef flatiron
   steak or sirloin, cut into
   2 x 1 x ½ strips
2 cups red onion,
   julienned
2 aji amarillo chile
   peppers, seeded,
   peeled, julienned
1 tablespoon red wine
   vinegar

1 teaspoon soy sauce
1 tablespoon cilantro,
   coarsely chopped
3 Roma or plum tomatoes,
   cut into wedges
1 pound yellow flesh
   potatoes, cut into
   3 x ¾ x ¾ pieces

4 ounces beef broth
2½ cups white rice,
   cooked
5-6 cilantro sprigs for
   garnish
1 tablespoon salt and 1
   tablespoon pepper,
   mixed
Vegetable oil, as needed

Blanch potatoes in oil (300°F) for 5 minutes or until soft. Drain with paper towels. In sauté pan (non-stick) heat oil and sear beef. Add 1½ tablespoons of salt and pepper mix. Sauté for 3 minutes or until you can't see juice from the beef. Then add onions and aji amarillo chile peppers. Sauté another 2 minutes. Add the rest of the salt and pepper mix and tomatoes. Add 1 tablespoon of chopped cilantro. Let that cook for 1 more minute then add beef broth, potatoes, soy sauce and red wine vinegar.

Serve with or over white rice and garnish with cilantro sprig.

Editor's Note: Aji amarillo Peruvian hot yellow peppers, also known as escabeche, are available at Latino markets.

Enjoy your delicious meal!

 Cabernet Sauvignon from Castello di Borghese has a deep ruby appearance with highly extracted flavors and moderate tannins. A rich start that tapers to a textured, rounded and well balanced finish.

Home of Fine Greek Cuisine

127-16 Smithtown Boulevard
Nesconset

Phone: 631-979-0924
Fax: 631-979-9806

Loucas K. Pericli, Owner/Chef

Credit Cards: amex, mc, and visa

Lunch: Monday - Saturday 11:00 am to 3:30 pm
Dinner: Monday - Thursday 3:30 pm - 10:00 pm
Friday and Saturday 3:30 pm - 11:00 pm
Closed Sunday

Since opening in 1989, this friendly, neighborhood favorite serves delicious and wholesome Mediterranean dishes tweaked for the American palate. This means that dill and anchovies must be requested for your Greek salad.

Don't get discouraged by the line of customers. It moves quickly, thanks to the addition of a back room to accommodate Loucas Pericli's many loyal and growing customers. If you prefer to take your meal home, all orders are available for take-out.

chicken mediterranean

Serves: 3-4

1 pound chicken cutlet
(cut in cubes)
2 fresh red tomatoes
(cut in cubes)
1 teaspoon crushed
garlic
1/2 cup olive oil

1 tablespoon fresh
chopped parsley
8 ounce cup crumbled
feta
1 tablespoon tomato
paste
1/4 cup chopped onion

2 tablespoons sherry
wine
1/2 teaspoon oregano
Black pepper

Heat the olive oil and cook the chicken (put aside).

In the same pan, sauté onions and garlic for 5 minutes, add wine and then add the tomatoes and parsley.

Cook for 5 minutes. Add the cooked chicken and simmer for another 5 minutes. Remove from heat and mix in feta.

Serve over rice.

 Cabernet Franc from Castello di Borghese has a racy style and is very pleasing.

THE AMERICAN HOTEL RESTAURANT

Located in The American Hotel

Main Street
Sag Harbor

Reservations Required - 631-725-3535
All Credit Cards Accepted

Open for Lunch and Dinner

Smart Casual Attire

Ted Conklin, Owner
Peter Dunlop, Executive Chef

www.theamericanhotel.com
e-mail: pk@theamericanhotel.com

Located in a historic Sag Harbor landmark, The American Hotel, this Zagat top rated restaurant features creative dishes that bring the enticing flavors of France, Italy, America and Asia to the tables. The Hotel and Restaurant are regarded by locals and visitors as one of the most elegant, charming and professionally run establishments on the East End of Long Island.

brandade de moreau (cod fish soufflé)

Serves: 10

2 ½ pounds salt cod
2 ½ pounds Yukon gold
    potatoes
10 ounces Spanish onion,
    chopped

4 ounces garlic
2 cups white wine
2 cups water
Sprig of fresh thyme

Bay leaf
2 cups crème fraiche
1 cup heavy cream
Salt and pepper to taste

Place first 8 ingredients in a pot and bring to a boil for 5 minutes. Strain and place into a mixing bowl.

Whip cod and potato mix on high speed.

Add crème fraiche, heavy cream, salt and pepper slowly.

Place soufflé mix under broiler until golden brown.

Serve with toast points and lemon.

French oak gives distinct character to Castello di Borghese Barrel Fermented Chardonnay and Pinot Noir which are both excellent food wines.

BARNEYS

restaurant

www.barneyslocustvalley.com

315 Buck Ram Road, Locust Valley
Tel: 516-671-6300

MITCHELL HAUSER, CHEF AND OWNER

Hours:
Monday - Thursday: 5:30 PM - 10 PM
Friday - Saturday: 5:30 PM - 11 PM
Sunday: 5:00 PM - 9 PM

Visa, MasterCard, American Express

This New American restaurant, nestled in historic Locust Valley, was once an old country inn. Since 1995, Mitchell and Deborah Hauser have created a warm and inviting place for you to enjoy a superb dinner. The style of cooking is classical French and American with highly innovative touches.

The dining rooms burst with inviting colors, fabrics, wallpapers, and other decorative touches. Deborah is a knowledgeable hunter of antiques and many of her treasures fill the restaurant. The inviting ensemble is often likened to an upstate country inn.

venison osso buco

Serves: 8 (2 pieces per person)

16 pieces venison osso buco
Flour to coat
Salt and pepper
Oil for sautéing
16 cloves garlic, peeled

2 Spanish onions, sliced
4 carrots, cut into ½ inch slices
8 plum tomatoes, quartered
1 bottle red wine

8 ounces red currant jelly
2 sprigs rosemary
1 quart beef stock or broth
1 large casserole pot

Heat oil, season osso buco with salt and pepper and dredge in flour. Brown on all sides. Remove from casserole. Add onions and carrots, sauté 5 minutes. Add garlic and 2 ounces flour, mix well and add red wine and currant jelly. Add tomatoes, rosemary and broth.

Return osso to pot, cover and place in 350°F oven for 1 ½ -2 hours or until tender.

Serve with wild rice or pasta.

Chef's Note: It's unique, yet can all be prepared a day ahead of time. Veal can be substituted for venison.

Editor's Note: Osso buco is traditionally a veal shank.

A rich red blend of mostly Cabernet Sauvignon, Castello di Borghese Meritage works well with this recipe.

BARRISTER'S

36 Main Street, Southampton
Tel: 631-283-6206 / Fax: 631-283-6230

MICHAEL FERRAN, OWNER
CAROL DALY, CHEF

Lunch and Sunday Brunch: 11:30 am - 4:00 pm
Dinner: 5:30 pm - 11:00 pm
"in between menu": 4:00 pm - 5:00 pm

Reservations required for parties of 6 or more

All major credit cards accepted

Located in the heart of Southampton Village, Barrister's has been a favorite of all ages for over twenty-five years. It is an affordable upscale family restaurant serving an eclectic mix of fresh local fish, salads, steaks, wraps and burgers. The dining room, bright and airy in the day and softly lit in the evenings, has a mix of locals and visitors all enjoying the food and comfort of the bar. The dress is casual.

grilled chicken & arugula salad with roasted red pepper-balsamic vinaigrette

Serves: 6

For Dressing
1 cup balsamic
   vinegar
2 ¼ cups olive oil
7 ounces diced pimientos
   or roasted red peppers
Salt and pepper to taste

For Salad
6 bunches of rinsed and
   dried arugula
6 6-ounce boneless,
   skinless chicken breasts

For Dressing
Combine all ingredients. Mix well and allow to refrigerate 4-6 hours.

For Salad
Grill, broil or bake chicken breasts.

To Serve
Divide arugula on six plates. Top with sliced chicken and 2 ounces of dressing.

Chef's Note: Customers never tire of it. The dressing goes perfectly with the peppery arugula.

The full taste, body and character of Castello di Borghese Cabernet Franc highlights the ingredients in this salad.

THE BAYPORT HOUSE

291 Bayport Avenue, Bayport

Phone: 631-472-2444
Fax: 631-472-5804

Executive Chef, Gerard Meade

Casual but neat attire

Lunch Weekdays
Noon - 2:30 pm

Dinner
Monday, Wednesday - Saturday: 5:00 pm
Sunday: 4:00 pm

Sunday Brunch
11 am - 2:30 pm

Happy Hour
Monday, Wednesday - Friday: 5-7 pm
Closed Tuesday

Corporate accounts and Gift Certificates available.
All major credit cards accepted.

New owners, Bill and Leda Sukow, have made this longtime Bayport eatery into a destination for creative New American food. The dishes are "innovative", "excellent", "diverse" and "well prepared". The service is "exceptional" and the decor demonstrates "old world charm" with modern "accents". The Bayport House is Zagat rated "Excellent" 2003-2004. Fridays and Saturdays it's "Frankie Piano" in the piano bar at 7:00 PM

horseradish crusted salmon filets

Serves: 4

4 salmon filets
   (boneless and skinless)
   approximately 1¼ -
   1 ½ inch thick
2 tablespoons whole
   grain mustard
1 piece (2-3 inches) fresh
   horseradish*, finely
   grated

Juice of one lemon (½ if
   using prepared
   horseradish)
Splash of white wine
Seasoned bread crumbs
   (fresh crumbs with a
   blend of fresh herbs,
   thyme, oregano and
   basil is best)

Kosher salt
Fresh black pepper

Season fish with salt and pepper. Blend mustard, horseradish, lemon juice and white wine in a mixing bowl. Add just enough bread crumbs to form a moist paste. Spread evenly over the fish just before cooking.

Wrap in foil and throw it on the grill for 8-10 minutes depending upon the thickness. (Make sure the barbecue is hot.)

If it is an oven you prefer, place salmon filets under broiler until browned and crisp.

Fresh spinach and rice are fine accompaniments.

If fresh horseradish is not available, substitute 1 ½ tablespoons prepared horseradish.

Chef's Note: This is a simple yet flavorful dish for any season.

Scrumptious with Castello di Borghese Cabernet Franc.

BELLES EAST

256 Elm Street, Southampton
Tel: 631-204-0300 / Fax: 631-204-9409

Jennifer and Tom McPadden, Owners
along with Linda Jones

A New Orleans Style Supper Club

Dinner 7 nights

Late night BBQ on weekends

This 100 year old landmark and site of the old Hansom House has been recreated to give the feel of a New Orleans bistro. Inside seats up to 100 people, while the popular outdoor patio and courtyard have enough seating for 75. Live music inside weeknights at 7:00 pm, weekends at 10:00 pm.

The menu offers Creole favorites including jambalayas, gumbos, and BBQ ribs, in addition to local fare such as fish, steak, chops and a raw bar. Make sure to save room for dessert as the dinner servings are very generous.

blackened fluke with cheese grits & greens

Serves: 1

Any firm fresh local
  fish cut to 8 ounce fillet,
  skin off
Melted butter

For Blackening Seasoning
1½ tablespoons cayenne
  pepper
1½ teaspoons onion
  powder
1½ teaspoons garlic
  powder
1 teaspoon kosher salt
1 teaspoon white pepper

1 teaspoon basil, dry
1 teaspoon thyme, dry
1 teaspoon oregano, dry
½ teaspoon cinnamon
1 tablespoon paprika

For Cheese Grit Cakes
1 cup quick grits
1 egg
1 cup sharp cheese
6 fresh basil leaves,
  chopped
¼ scallion, chopped
2 cups water

2 cups milk
Dash garlic powder
Salt and pepper to taste
4-6 dashes of tabasco

For Greens
Baby arugula
Olive oil
Salt and pepper to taste
Fresh lemon juice

Dip fish in melted butter. Coat with blackening seasoning. Place fish in smokin' hot cast iron pan. Sear on one side. Flip over. Finish in hot 500°F oven for 5 minutes.

Cheese Grit Cakes
Boil water and milk. Add all ingredients except egg. Cook and stir for 5 minutes. Let cool. Add beaten egg. Place in greased baking pan. Place in 350°F oven for 15 minutes. Let set for 5 minutes and then cut to your liking.

Combine arugula, olive oil, salt, pepper, and lemon juice. Toss quickly. Pile greens on center of plate. Place fish on top of greens. Garnish with your favorite salsa. Add grit cakes on the plate. Ready to serve.

Instinct might be to pick a white wine but blackened or grilled fish pair beautifully with Castello di Borghese Cabernet Franc.

www.bistrocassis.com

55 B Wall Street, Huntington
Tel: 631-421-4122 / Fax: 631-421-4078

Julio Velaske, Chef

Casual Attire

Lunch
Monday - Saturday Noon - 3:00 pm

Dinner
Monday - Thursday, Sunday 5:00 pm - 10:00 pm
Friday, Saturday 5:00 pm - 11:00 pm

Brunch
Sunday 11:00 am - 3:00 pm

All Major Credit Cards Accepted

Bistro Cassis brings a warm touch of Gallic charm and superb French food to Long Island's Huntington Village. Its ambience and décor are reminders of the smoky bistros celebrated in French film noir. Enter the dining room and its carved cherry pilasters, ornate tin ceiling, soaring marble pillars and outsize antique mirrors transport you to the Parisian Left Bank. The intimate atmosphere of this unparalleled French restaurant combines a quiet elegance with a welcoming, unpretentious spirit.

Its menu reads like a bistro and brasserie hall of fame, with its salade frisee aux ladons, salade nicoise, soupe a l'oignon, moules Provencales, steak frites, coq au vin, boeuf bourguignon, crème brulee and tart au Citron. On Friday nights, a guitarist and singer fill the air with French ("La Vie en Rose") and American ("Blue Moon") songs.

Bistro Cassis offers a taste of Gallic charm you'll long remember.

pan seared scallops and shrimp with fricassee of oyster mushroom and leeks

Serves: 4

12 sea scallops
12 jumbo shrimp
2 Portobello mushrooms,
   ground
½ pound oyster
   mushrooms, sliced
½ pound leeks, sliced

1 cup heavy cream
2 tablespoons butter
2 tablespoons oil
1 tablespoon truffle oil
Salt and white pepper,
   to taste

For the Fricassee
Heat the oil in a wide sauté pan. Add the oyster mushrooms and sauté them for a few minutes, then add the leeks. Cook for another 2 minutes, then add 1 tablespoon of butter and season with salt and white pepper to taste.

For the Sauce
In a small saucepan, heat the ground Portobello mushrooms in oil, cook for 3 minutes. Add the heavy cream, reduced about 5 minutes and finish it with 1 tablespoon of butter, truffle oil, salt and pepper to taste.

For the Scallops and Shrimp
Heat the oil in a large sauté pan. Season the scallops and the shrimp, sauté them for a few minutes on each side. Serve immediately.

Presentation
Cover each dinner plate with sauce. Place a portion of fricassee in center of the plates, alternating the shrimp and scallops around the fricassee. Serve immediately.

Castello di Borghese Founders' Field Sauvignon Blanc Reserve will enhance this full flavored yet delicate recipe. You could also pair it with Estate Chardonnay.

1362 OLD NORTHERN BOULEVARD
ROSLYN VILLAGE
516-403-4400
www.bistrocitron.com

HOURS:
Lunch
Monday - Friday Noon - 3:00 pm
Dinner
Sunday - Thursday 5:00 pm - 10:00 pm
Friday, Saturday 5:00 pm - 11:00 pm
Brunch
Saturday Noon - 3:00 pm
Sunday 11:00 am - 3:00 pm

Pierre Landet, Chef
Casual Attire
All Major Credit Cards Accepted

Dine on authentic classics served in the finest French restaurants as well as simple country comfort food - Moules Provencales, Salade Nicoise, Soupe a l'Oignon, Steak Frites, Coq au Vin, Boeuf Bourguignon, Crème Brulee and Tart au Citron. The staff provides impeccable service and is knowledgeable in every aspect of the restaurant's food and wine selections.

For an intimate meal, a special occasion, or just for dessert and coffee; Bistro Citron offers the best of the Old World in today's world.

butter poached maine lobster & monk fish loin with julienne vegetables and mustard spaetzle

Serves: 2

1¼ pound fresh Maine
   lobster
2 monkfish loins,
   approximately 1 pound
   each
1 zucchini
2 yellow squash
2 medium carrots

For Stock
1 carrot
1 onion
1 stalk of celery

1 clove of garlic
1 tomato

For Mustard Spaetzle
2 eggs, beaten
2 cups flour, sifted
1 cup milk
2 tablespoons turmeric
Salt and pepper to taste
3 teaspoons Pommery
   mustard
⅛ cup fresh parsley

1 tablespoon Dijon
   mustard
1 tablespoon curry
   powder
Olive oil

For Sauce
2 cups lobster stock
1 tablespoon arrowroot
3 sprigs of fresh thyme
2 tablespoons water, or
   brandy, if desired

To a pot of boiling salted water, add carrots, onion, celery, garlic, and tomato and cook about 20 minutes. Add lobster and thyme and continue cooking 12 minutes. Remove lobster and reserve all the strained stock. Thicken about 1/2 cup of the stock with arrowroot (mix a little arrowroot with a little brandy or cold water, then add to stock) and bring to a boil. Reserve this sauce.

Cut vegetables into thin strips. Blanch vegetables separately in salted water until vegetables are al dente, approximately 30 seconds. Plunge in ice water to halt cooking, reserve for later use.

Combine eggs, parsley, and flour. Add enough milk to the flour to form a stiff batter. Add tumeric, salt, pepper, Pommery mustard, Dijon mustard, and curry powder. Using a rubber spatula, push batter through a colander into pan of simmering salted water. Cook spaetzle until they rise to the surface, then remove with a slotted spoon and plunge them into ice water. Drain again. When cool toss with olive oil.

Unshell the lobster, cut the tail in two, remove the claws and place in remainder of stock (not used for sauce). Add about 2 tablespoons of butter to this stock.

Clean monkfish, form the long pieces into a spiral and secure with a toothpick. Brown in olive oil until cooked, remove from pan and add the spaetzle to the same pan with the drippings.

Assemble the dish placing the spaetzle and vegetables on the plate and top with the monkfish. Drizzle the fish with the reserved sauce and place lobster pieces on top. Garnish with fresh basil.

Castello di Borghese Barrel Fermented Chardonnay tastes heavenly with Maine lobster. Try it!

B.K. Sweeney's Parkside Tavern

356 Broadway, Bethpage
Tel: 516-935-9597 / Fax: 516-935-9604

www.bksweeneys.com

Hours
Sunday, Monday 11:30 am - 10:00 pm
Tuesday - Thursday 11:30 am - 11:00 pm
Friday, Saturday 11:30 am- 12:00 am

GARY ABBONDOLA, CHEF

Reservations required for parties of 8 or more

Casual Attire

All Major Credit Cards Accepted

B.K. Sweeney's Parkside Tavern functions as the main gathering place for many Bethpagers and visitors to the area. In the heart of the village, the tavern suggests a cozy English pub with rich oak appointments and dark green accents.

The food is delicious and hearty. Super steaks, homemade chicken pot pies, pastas, and fresh seafood head the menu and may be ordered at the bar or at your table.

This upscale establishment is child-friendly and family-oriented.

shrimp scampi

Serves: 1

1 ½ ounces olive oil
1 teaspoon garlic, minced
7 shrimp (16-20)*, tail on
2 ounces butter
2 ounces white wine
1 teaspoon capers
1 teaspoon lemon juice

6 ounces fish or clam
    stock
8 ounces linguine,
    pre-cooked (al dente)
½ teaspoon salt
1 tablespoon parsley,
    chopped

Garnish with 1 teaspoon
    parsley

Precook pasta in pasta boiler. Put 1 ounce olive oil, butter, minced garlic, capers and lemon juice in saute pan. Heat until garlic is golden brown. Add shrimp, deglaze with white wine, and let reduce. Add clam or fish stock and a pinch of salt. When pasta is done "al dente," add it to the pan, add chopped parsley, and ½ ounce olive oil. Toss and mix well. Taste and adjust if you need to. Arrange on 12 inch pasta bowl. Garnish with remaining 1 teaspoon parsley.

Editor's Note: 16-20 shrimp per pound refers to extra large shrimp.

This dish begs for a Chardonnay. Try the Castello di Borghese Estate or, if you want a more full bodied wine, the Barrel Fermented Chardonnay is buttery, creamy and in complete harmony with this recipe.

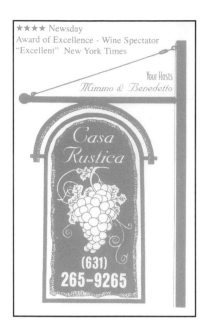

175 West Main Street, Smithtown

Tel: 631-265-9265

www.casarustica.net

Benedetto Gambino, Chef/Owner

Reservations Suggested

Lunch
Monday - Friday: 12 noon - 3 pm
Dinner
Monday - Friday 5 pm - 10 pm
Saturday 5 - 11 pm
Sunday 2 - 9 pm

All major credit cards accepted

"Smithtown's Casa Rustica is a champion among Italian restaurants on an island loaded with contenders. A look at the menu and a taste of the food separate Casa Rustica from the pack. Many of its most distinctive dishes are not found elsewhere on Long Island."
- The New York Times

veal casa rustica

Serves: 1

1 veal cutlet
Flavored bread crumbs
½ cup canola oil
1 egg
½ cup flour

For Tomato Salad
3 plum tomatoes
6 basil leaves
1 cup fresh arugula
Olive oil and balsamic
  vinegar to taste

2 cloves of garlic
¼ cup red onions,
  chopped
2 pieces of fresh
  mozzarella

Dredge veal cutlet in flour, then egg and into bread crumbs. Get a pan with ½ cup of canola oil. Put in on the fire. Wait until hot. Then fry cutlet until golden brown on both sides. Set aside.

For Salad
Cut tomatoes, arugula, basil and garlic. Place in a mixing bowl. Add olive oil and balsamic vinegar and red onions. Mix. Add salt and pepper to taste. Place veal on a plate. Put the salad on top and enjoy. If you like mozzarella, melt it on top of veal cutlet before adding the salad.

Chef's Note: It's quick, simple and delicious!

Bon Appetite!

 Excellent with Pinot Noir Reserve or Barrel Fermented Chardonnay.

COLLINS & MAIN

100 Old South Main Street
Sayville

Reservations Suggested Weekends - 631-563-0805

All Credit Cards Accepted

Vincent Malizion, Jerry Marlow, Owners
Anthony Russo, Executive Chef

www.collinsandmain.com

Lunch
Tuesday - Friday Noon - 2:30 pm
Dinner
Tuesday - Friday 5:00 pm - 9:30 pm
Saturday 5:00 pm - 10:00 pm
Sunday Private Parties Only
Closed Mondays

Located in the heart of the picturesque Village of Sayville, this restaurant blends sophistication with neighborhood friendliness. Enjoy live music weekends in the piano lounge before dining on New American cuisine in the main dining room. Tastefully decorated with pale yellow walls and wood accenting, the dining room is adorned with large photos of old Sayville, giving it a minimalist feel. There is something for everyone at this culinary delight.

filet mignon medallions/sliced shiitake mushroom port wine demi glaze

Serves: 4

4 pieces of 4 ounce filet
   mignon
1 cup sliced shiitake
   mushrooms
4 ounces port wine
3 pieces roasted garlic

6 ounces veal stock
4 tablespoons extra-virgin
   olive-oil
¼ pound butter
Salt and pepper to taste

Season filet mignon with salt and pepper. Place to side.

Melt butter in large sauté pan.

Place medallions into the melted butter, 2 minutes on each side. Set them aside.

Add roasted garlic and sliced shiitake, then add port wine.

Bring to a boil, lower heat, simmer until wine is reduced by ½ , then add veal stock.

Place filet mignon in sauce until you reach desired temperature.

Chef's Note: Place filet mignon over potato puree with vegetables. Add port sauce.

Castello di Borghese Merlot Reserve is complex, intense and well balanced just like this recipe.

located inside The Inn at East Wind

5720 Route 25A
Wading River

Phone 631-846-2335, Fax 631-929-4975
Reservations Recommended

www.theinnateastwind.com

Rich Laurelli, Chef

Restaurant and Pub Open Seven Days a Week
Sunday-Thursday, 8 am-9 pm
Friday and Saturday, 8 am-10:00 pm
Bar Hours Open Late

All Major Credit Cards Accepted

We offer a variety of dining to suit any mood. Our fine dining restaurant provides guests with an elegant setting in which to enjoy a delicious array of world-class cuisine. Mahogany paneled walls, a 24-foot bar and a comfortable, private setting set the tone for a relaxing breakfast, lunch or dinner experience.

For a more casual atmosphere, our Pub serves a lively and inventive menu of light fare favorites and offers a hip yet casual environment, making it the perfect spot to gather with friends. Ultra plush and comfortable, the lounge offers a relaxed atmosphere where guests can enjoy drinks, entertainment and more. Weekend entertainment and daily specials are always available.

sautéed soft shell crabs with brown hazelnut butter & ripe cherry tomatoes

Serves: 1

2 soft shell crabs,
    cleaned
Kosher salt and fresh
    ground pepper, to taste
1 cup flour
1 tablespoon Old Bay
    Seasoning
2 shallots, thinly sliced

2 tablespoons whole
    sweet butter
1/4 cup chopped hazelnuts
Pinch of fresh thyme,
    chopped
1/2 cup white wine
Juice of 1 fresh lemon
3 cherry tomatoes, halved

Heat skillet with clarified butter. Season crabs with kosher salt and fresh ground pepper. Dredge crabs in flour seasoned with Old Bay Seasoning. (Tip: poke crabs with a fork before sautéing to avoid splattering.) Sauté crabs on both sides until brown, then remove from pan and discard butter.

In same pan, add 2 shallots, thinly sliced, with 2 tablespoons of whole sweet butter. Add 1/4 cup of chopped hazelnuts and cook until shallots are fully cooked and butter is beginning to brown. Combine thyme, white wine, and lemon juice and add to pan. Place crabs back in pan and simmer with 3 cherry tomatoes, halved, for about 4 minutes until crabs are fully cooked.

Chef's Note: At Desmond's we serve this dish with local braising greens and crispy shoe string potatoes.

Castello di Borghese's signature wine is Pinot Noir. I like to think of it as an all occasion wine because it pairs equally well with seafood, light meat and light pastas. If you're in the mood for red and the food is on the lighter side, try Pinot Noir.

THE GRILL ROOM

160 Adams Avenue, Hauppauge
Tel: 631-436-7330 / Fax: 631-436-5048

A.J. Cataffo, Proprietor
Bryan Zembreski, Executive Chef

Eclectic Cuisine

Hours
Monday - Thursday: 11:30 am - 10:30 pm
Friday: 11:30 pm - 11:30 pm
Saturday: 6:00 pm - 11:30 pm

Reservations Recommended
Visa, MC, AmEx, and Diner's card accepted

Enjoy live music every Friday evening
Catering is available

"Who woulda thunk it?" ask admirers about this "respite in the middle of an industrial park", where a "cool", "loft-like" room full of "candles, live music (weekend nights) and beautiful people" equals a "little slice of NYC" in Hauppauge; the "daring, cosmopolitan" eclectic menu yields "excellent" dishes, the staff's "terrific" and the ambiance is "romantic".

macadamia encrusted arctic char toasted orzo pasta

Serves: 5

1 arctic char* 2-4 pounds filet boned, skin on, portioned

Fish
1 cup macadamia nuts, medium chopped
1/2 cup panko (Japanese) bread crumbs
1/4 teaspoon ground coriander
2 egg whites
1 cup flour

Salt and pepper to taste

Orzo Pasta
1 cup raw orzo pasta
3 cups chicken stock
1 tablespoon butter
1/4 cup grated Romano

Lemon Ginger Aioli
1 cup mayonnaise
2 lemon zest/juice
1 tablespoon grated fresh ginger

1 teaspoon ground ginger
1 teaspoon honey
1 tablespoon Dijon mustard
Salt and pepper to taste

Bok Choy
6 heads baby bok choy (cut in quarters)
2 tablespoons butter
1 tablespoon sesame oil
Salt and pepper to taste

Fish
Mix macadamia nuts, bread crumbs and coriander together. Dip filet in flour, egg, then macadamia mixture. Cook in sauté pan half butter, half oil. Brown crust. Finish in 400°F oven for 4 minutes. Remove skin and serve.

Orzo Pasta
In sauce pot, toast orzo pasta on low heat with butter. Add half chicken stock until dry, then add remaining stock. Cook until dry over medium heat. Finish with cheese.

Lemon Ginger Aioli
Mix all ingredients together. Let mix sit in refrigerator overnight (can be held for a week).

Bok Choy
Boil large pot of salted water. Blanch bok choy about 4-5 minutes. Melt butter in saute pan with sesame oil. Strain bok choy. Toss bok choy with butter and sesame oil. Season with salt and pepper.

Presentation
Place three bok choy in triangle in the center of the plate. Place orzo pasta in the middle to fill the triangle, then add the Arctic char, encrusted side up, on top of the orzo pasta. Add lemon ginger aioli dots around the perimeter of the plate and garnish with chives.

*substitution fish: salmon

 To really bring together the exotic flavors of this dish pair Castello di Borghese Estate Chardonnay.

H2O
SEAFOOD · GRILL

215 West Main Street, Smithtown

Phone: 631-361-6464
Fax: 631-979-7998

www.h2oseafoodgrill.com

MICHAEL BOHLSEN, OWNER
SCOTT SZEKRETAR, CHEF

Open 7 Days a week for Dinner
Monday - Wednesday, 5:00 pm - 10:00 pm
Thursday - Saturday 5:00 pm - 11:00 pm
Sunday - 2:00 pm - 9:00 pm

All major credit cards accepted

H2O Restaurant gracefully delivers a classic seafood house, all the while embracing the aesthetic of a contemporary American grill. The contemporary bar features an 18 foot ceiling and leads to an adjacent dining room that is perfect for private parties up to 40 people.

The H2O menu features a raw bar, all sizes of hard shell lobsters, simple grilled fish, and prime steaks. H2O also prides itself on the Sushi Bar which creates the most authentic and exciting sushi and sashimi on Long Island.

sesame seared tuna

Serves: 2

8 ounces fresh sushi grade tuna

Black and white sesame seeds to coat

3 tablespoons honey soy sauce (2 tablespoons honey to 1 tablespoon soy sauce mixed until incorporated)

2 ounces sticky rice (½ cup sushi rice, 1 cup water, 1 ounce rice wine vinegar, ½ ounce sugar)

Prepared wasabi to garnish

For Sticky Rice

Rinse sushi rice and put in a pot with the 1 cup water. Cover and bring to a boil. Reduce heat to a simmer. Cook until the water is absorbed (about 20 minutes) and let rest for 5 minutes. Combine the sugar and vinegar in a bowl. Add the rice and toss to incorporate the vinegar mixture. Set rice aside.

Roll tuna in the sesame seed mixture. In a hot pan with oil, sear the tuna for about 20 seconds on each side. Tuna should be very rare and seeds should stick to the tuna.

Slice the tuna about ⅛ inch thick and place on plate in a fan.

Work rice with hands to form a 2 ounce ball and place on the plate near top of the tuna fan.

Garnish with wasabi and with a spoon, drizzle honey soy sauce over top of the tuna. Serve and enjoy.

Castello di Borghese Founders' Field Sauvignon Blanc Reserve is made from the oldest vines on Long Island. The reserve has about 20% French oak and is loaded with flavors of honeysuckle, mangos, melons and tropical fruit. This wine will transport you!

Irish Coffee Pub

restaurant • catering • entertainment

131 CARLTON AVENUE, EAST ISLIP
TEL: 631-277-0007 / FAX: 631-277-4744

www.irishcoffeepub.com

Chefs
Leo Harrington, Brian Lam, John Bulanchuck

Owners
Fred Billings, Leo Harrington, Fintan Stapleton,
Stephan Mahood, Niall Kelly

Restaurant Hours
Monday - Thursday 11:30 am - 10:00 pm
Friday 11:30 am - 11:00 pm
Saturday 5:00 pm - 11:00 pm
Sunday 1:00 pm - 9:00 pm

Much more than a pub…

Located in the heart of East Islip, the Irish Coffee Pub is one of Long Island's most elegant restaurants and catering facilities. From the beautiful brass railed sweeping staircase, gently lighted by Waterford Crystal chandeliers, to our manicured and picturesque gardens, the Irish Coffee Pub is richly decorated with professional service and delicious food selections.

salmon o'brien

Serves: 4

4 8-ounce salmon filets	*Cajun Lobster Beurre*	1 cup white wine
½ onion, sliced paper thin	*Blanc Sauce*	½ cup lobster stock
3 eggs	⅛ teaspoon Cajun season	
2 cups flour	4 tablespoons flour	
4 to 5 tablespoons of oil	4 tablespoons butter	
	½ cup heavy cream	

Dredge salmon and onion in flour. Heat 4-5 tablespoons oil in sauté pan. Add 2 small amounts of floured onion in pan, side by side. Dip salmon filet in egg wash and place on top of onions. Cook until golden on both sides. Repeat with other 2 pieces. Place salmon on small sheet pan and finish cooking in 350°F oven until cooked through.

Cajun Lobster Beurre Blanc Sauce
In small sauté pan reduce white wine by half. Add heavy cream and lobster stock. Bring to a boil, then reduce heat. Add Cajun seasons. Thicken sauce with a roux. (To make roux, melt butter in sauté pan, whisk in flour, cook until golden.) Add hot roux slowly to sauce until desired thickness.

Castello di Borghese's first wine released with the new label was the Barrel Fermented Chardonnay. An elegant core of lemon, pear and citrus flavors - it has a long lingering finish.

The Jolly Fisherman & Steak House

AMERICAN SEAFOOD & STEAK

25 MAIN STREET
ROSLYN
516-621-0055

Fred and Steven Scheiner, Owners
Steven Scheiner, Executive Chef

Casual Neat Attire

HOURS:
Lunch: Tuesday - Saturday Noon - 3:00 pm
Dinner: Tuesday - Saturday 4:30 pm - close
Sunday - 1 pm - 9 pm

Reservations Suggested

All Major Credit Cards Accepted

After 47 years of serving the freshest seafood, The Jolly Fisherman has become known as the "King Fish of L.I. Seafood Restaurants."

Opened in 1957 by Fred Scheiner, The Jolly Fisherman overlooks beautiful Silver Lake in the heart of Old Roslyn. Customers can enjoy elegant lake view dining, or intimate fireside tables with top-notch service by a knowledgeable, tuxedo-clad waitstaff.

Specialties include live Maine lobster stuffed with shrimp, scallops, and mushrooms; macadamia nut crusted Atlantic salmon; and pan-seared Chilean sea bass with roasted garlic sauce. There are no shortcuts taken here. Everything is homemade, from the soups, dressings and sauces, to the fabulous desserts. An appreciation for this has kept customers returning year after year.

macadamia-nut crusted salmon with red bean salsa

Serves: 4

4 portions of fresh
  salmon filet (8 ounces
  each)
1 cup raw macadamia
  nuts, chopped fine
1 spanish onion,
  sliced thin
4 tablespoons honey
  and 1 tablespoon Dijon
  mustard combined

Dry Ingredients
3 tablespoons flour
1 teaspoon sugar
1 teaspoon paprika
1 pinch cayenne
1 pinch salt
Fresh ground pepper

Salsa
1 24-ounce can red kidney
  beans (drained)
1 ½ tablespoons extra
  virgin olive oil

1 tablespoon each:
  (finely diced)
  green pepper
  red pepper
  yellow pepper
  red onion
1 clove garlic, finely
  minced
Salt and fresh pepper to
  taste

Toss sliced onion in a bowl with the six dry ingredients.

Fry in canola oil until very crisp. Remove and let dry on paper towels for ½ hour.

Preheat oven to 350°F.

Chop the fried onion fine, then combine with the macadamia nuts.

Place 4 salmon portions on a cookie sheet. Skin side down, paint the top of each with the honey/mustard mixture. Sprinkle the onion/nut mixture evenly over the salmon.

Bake at 350°F for 12-15 minutes.

For salsa: combine all ingredients in a bowl.

Excellent with Pinot Noir Reserve from Castello di Borghese.

KABUL GRILL
KABOB & TEA HOUSE

129 North Broadway, Hicksville
Tel: 516-933-8999 / Fax: 516-933-8998

Afghani Cuisine specializing in a variety of kabobs

Trina Shair, Chef and Owner

Credit Cards: Visa, MC, AmEx

casual, neat attire

reservations recommended

Hours
Monday- Saturday: Noon - 11:00 pm
Sunday: 3:00 pm - 11:00 pm

"The shimmering, striking Kabul Grill in Hicksville is a jewel of a restaurant that offers a seductive, romantic atmosphere and penny-wise process. The highlight of this serene new Afghan spot is the archways that line the walls; at night when each of them is illuminated by a torch-shaped sconce that casts a subdued glow, they evoke visions of mosques and minarets."
- The New York Times

lawand chicken breast with chef's rich, special gravy

Serves: 4

1 medium size onion (chopped very fine)

1 teaspoon crushed garlic

1 ½ pounds of chicken breast (2 large pieces) cut into small square chunks

16 ounce container sour cream

4 tablespoons olive oil

1 teaspoon salt

2 teaspoons coriander powder

A touch of red powdered chili (depending on how hot you want)

¼ tablespoon curry powder

½ bunch chopped fresh cilantro (or as much as desired)

Put oil and very finely chopped onion in a pot and let simmer at medium temperature on a stove, until onion becomes gold. Then add garlic and chicken. Stir (sauté) for 3 minutes. Add all spices (seasonings) and stir for another 2 minutes. Add one cup of water. Cover pot and let cook for 5 minutes until water is gone. Add sour cream and fresh chopped cilantro, stir and mix and let cook for 15 minutes, do not cover pot anymore. Serve hot in a deep dish. Sprinkle some cilantro on top for taste and decoration.

Chef's Note: Lawand has a unique and delicious taste. It is filling without being overpowering. It is served best with Basmati white rice. It can be made ahead of time and frozen. Lawand must be defrosted with stove head (put in a pan over stove and let thaw). Ingredients cannot be substituted.

Castello di Borghese Riesling, tart and fruity wine, is a wonderful match for the chicken with red pepper and curry.

NEAPOLITAN CUISINE

400 Furrows Road, Holbrook
Tel: 631-737-0774 / Fax: 631-737-6784

www.mammalombardis.com

Guy Lombardi, Chef

Open seven days a week
Sunday-Thursday 11:30 am - 10 pm
Friday and Saturday 11:30 am - 11:30 pm

All Major Credit Cards Accepted

As you pass our scenic garden, the sounds of opera will draw you into our elegant dining room. Here you will feast on homemade, authentic Neapolitan recipes that the Lombardi family has carefully prepared for generations.

Professional, personal service, robust flavors, and generous portions set the standards for this family owned restaurant where "Reputation is Everything". Our award winning wine list and the finest Southern Italian cuisine will turn any occasion, including catering and accommodations for large parties, into a special and memorable event.

La vita é bella - mangia!

lobster meat in brodetto over angel hair

Serves: 1 to 2

1/4 **pound of lobster meat (cooked and shelled)**
1 **cup of Italian tomatoes in juice**
8-10 **fresh grape tomatoes**
1/2 **cup of white wine**

1/2 **cup of clear seafood broth or clam juice**
5 **leaves of fresh chopped basil**
3 **cloves of garlic, diced**
3 **tablespoons of olive oil**
Salt to taste

Pepper to taste
1/2 **pound "DeCecco" angel hair pasta**

In a saucepan, sauté olive oil and garlic until garlic is lightly browned.

Add the white wine, seafood broth, tomatoes in juice, grape tomatoes, basil, salt and pepper and let simmer in the sauce pan for ten minutes.

Then add the cooked lobster meat and simmer for an additional five minutes.

In a separate pot, boil water and add angel hair pasta. Boil until cooked to your preference.

Remove and strain pasta and put in a large pasta bowl. Pour the lobster sauce over the pasta, garnish with fresh basil leaves and serve immediately.

Mangia and Enjoy!

Castello di Borghese Barrel Fermented Chardonnay is pure satisfaction.

PAZZO CUCINA

Italian Cuisine

**208 Route 112, Port Jefferson Station
Tel: 631-473-2085**

www.pazzocucina.com

ANGELO GALEOTAFIORE, OWNER/CHEF

Hours
Tuesday - Sunday 5:00 pm- 10:00 pm

Credit cards: Visa, MC, AmEx, Diner's

*At Pazzo Cucina we are serious about feeding you
the most flavorful of creations.*

chilean sea bass alla lucia

Serves: 4

2 Portobello mushrooms (large cap 6 inch), chopped up small

½ Spanish onion (2 ounces - diced up really small)

1 garlic clove, small, minced

1 large tomato, chopped small

½ ounce Italian parsley

2 ounces Rhine wine

2 ounces extra virgin olive oil

4 8-ounce pieces of Chilean sea bass, deboned

4 ounces seasoned bread crumbs

Preheat oven to 425°F convection or 500°F regular oven.

Heat skillet until hot, add extra virgin olive oil, then garlic and onion, stir frequently. After 1 minute, add mushrooms and tomatoes, cook until most liquid has evaporated.

Add Rhine wine. Reduce liquid until wine evaporates - remove from heat. Add salt and pepper to taste, add Italian parsley, mix well and taste for flavor cohesiveness.

Cool down and refrigerate for later use or just cool down and add to sea bass in the following manner: Oil ovenproof dish and place sea bass onto dish. Take one scoop of mushroom mix and place on top of sea bass, spread evenly about ¼ inch thickness. Sprinkle bread crumbs on top of mushroom mix, sprinkle evenly about ½ ounce.

Drizzle extra virgin olive oil lightly on top of mushroom mix - ready for oven. Place sea bass into hot oven and cook for 10-12 minutes for a golden brown roasted look. Serve with lemon wedge.

Chef's Note: Serve with roasted asparagus and potatoes. The marriage of sea bass with Lucia's ingredients is "gastro"- amore!

Barrel Fermented Chardonnay encourages the flavors in this main dish to delight your palate.

Piccolo Ristorante

ITALIAN CUISINE

2770 SUNRISE HIGHWAY
BELLMORE

Phone: 516-679-8787

Thomas T. Valenti and Robert Valenti/Owners
Thomas J. Valenti/Chef

www.piccoloristorante.com

American Express, Visa, MasterCard

Hours:
Sunday - Thursday 11:00 am - 10:00 pm
Friday and Saturday 11:00 am - 11:00 pm

Since 1979 this award winning family business has provided unparalled combinations of Italian food, service, and value while expanding this unique restaurant three times to better accommodate ALL the special dining needs you deserve. Tom or Rob Valenti are always on hand to plan your next affair at Piccolo, your home or one of their satellite locations.

chicken michelangelo

Serves: 4 to 5

8 large tenderized chicken cutlets (pound them to your desired thinness)
1 pint of ricotta cheese
1 pound shredded Grande whole milk mozzarella cheese
2 cups chopped crimini mushrooms

1 cup sliced crimini mushrooms
½ cup of Romano grated cheese
½ cup granulated garlic
½ cup black pepper
3 cups heavy cream
1 tablespoon chicken base

1 tablespoon roux
¾ cup fresh puréed tomatoes
¼ cup oregano
¼ cup fresh finely chopped basil
¼ cup parsley

After cutlet is fried to a LITE golden brown consistency, place a smear (a smear is the male twin brother of the dollop with a little more panache, same weight, it just covers a little more ground) of chopped crimini mushrooms blended into seasoned (sprinkle in lightly some grated Romano cheese, granulated garlic and a dash of black pepper) ricotta on top of your breasts (chicken cutlet breasts, stay focused) then lightly cover the smears with shredded Grande mozzarella cheese. Bake in oven at 400°F for about 8-10 minutes until cheese melts evenly and ricotta is nice and hot.

While the chicken bakes we will prepare the sauce. Pour the heavy cream, diced mushrooms, roux (a 50-50 split of congealed flour and butter), puréed fresh tomatoes, chicken base, oregano, basil and parsley into your sauté pan. Stir intermittingly. Serve with the sauce poured over the finished chicken.

Chef's Note: Starting with the traditional first home cooked meal mastered, a basic breaded and fried chicken cutlet, this dish combines old school familiarity with a unique blend of comfort ingredients. For Atkins and South Beach fans, grilled chicken breasts may be substituted.

Editor's Note: Chicken base, found in most supermarkets, is a very thick substance that is often mixed with hot water to make a chicken stock.

Castello di Borghese Merlot, a silky smooth wine, complements this dish perfectly.

1 First Street, East Patchogue
Tel: 631-475-9843 / Fax: 631-475-9845

www.pinegroveinn.com

MICHAEL RIZZI, OWNER
LAWRENCE RUPP, CHEF

Lunch:
Tuesday - Saturday: 11:30 AM - 3:00 PM
Dinner:
Tuesday - Saturday: 3:00 PM - 10:00 PM
Sunday: Noon - 9:00 PM

Visa, MasterCard, American Express, Discover

Established in 1910, The Pine Grove Inn continues its tradition of fine food and service featuring a continental and American menu emphasizing fresh, seasonal ingredients. Every Saturday night at 7:30 pm, guests are treated to the voice of Jacques LeBas as he sings Frank Sinatra tunes. Happy Hour in the Pavilion Room is a must from 4 pm-7 pm every Friday.

porcini dusted diver sea scallops in a creole mustard cream sauce

Serves: 4

4 dried porcini mushrooms - pulverized into a fine powder

12 jumbo sea scallops, abductor muscle removed

12 ounces 40% heavy cream

1 tablespoon Dijon mustard

1 tablespoon horseradish root, freshly grated-fine

1 Roma tomato, skinned, seeded, ribs removed, julienned and diced small

4 ounces seaweed blanched, cooled in an ice bath

Sea salt to taste

White pepper, freshly ground to taste

Extra virgin olive oil (enough to barely coat the pan)

Clarified butter (same amount as olive oil)

Scallops
Take the scallops, season them with salt and white pepper, and place them in the porcini dust on one of the flat sides. In a moderately pre-heated non-stick sauté pan, add the extra virgin olive oil, the clarified butter and the scallops dusted side down. Sauté until colored very deeply and turn. Cook undusted side until golden brown.

Sauce
In a sauce pan, reduce the cream by half. Stir in the Dijon mustard and grated horseradish. Adjust seasoning with sea salt and white pepper to taste.

Presentation
Pool the sauce around a center pile of the seaweed, place 3 scallops, dusted side up, equidistant from each other and drop some diced tomato between the scallops.

Editor's Note: Clarified butter cooks at higher temperatures without browning and burning. It is made by slowly melting butter, skimming off the foam that rises to the top and then gently pouring the butter into a dish, leaving the milk solids behind.

Castello di Borghese Barrel Fermented Chardonnay and this recipe are a taste bud nirvana.

www.pomodorohuntington.com

62 Stewart Avenue, Huntington
Tel: 631-549-7074

Andrea Montello, Chef

Lunch
Monday - Friday: Noon - 3 pm
Dinner
Monday - Thursday: 4 pm - 10 pm
Friday and Saturday: 5 pm - 11 pm
Sunday: 5 pm - 10 pm

All major credit cards accepted
Reservations recommended for groups of five or more

Neat Attire

"Italian gems", these trattoria triplets offer "robust", "superbly prepared meals", and "warm" service in a setting styled after a café in Tuscany"; followers find them "reliable, pleasant" and "good on the wallet".

Born over a decade ago, the Huntington trattoria called Pomodoro was one of the first in what has become a mini-empire of restaurants, extending from Long Island to Manhattan. What's kept Pomodoro alive becomes clear at first bite: robust food, served in unpretentious red-checkered tablecloth surroundings.

seared red snapper served with basil mashed potatoes & roasted tomato coulis

Serves: 1

1 red snapper filet, deboned	**2 diver scallops**
5 ounces Yukon gold mashed potatoes	**2 Roma tomatoes**
	5 tablespoons extra-virgin Olive oil
1 tablespoon pesto	

Slice the Roma tomatoes in halves and roast them in a preheated oven at 350°F with a dash of oil, salt and pepper. Cook them for 10 minutes, then put them in a blender with 2 tablespoons of extra-virgin olive oil; once blended set aside.

Preheat a Teflon fry pan with 2 tablespoons extra-virgin olive oil. Put the red snapper previously seasoned with salt and pepper skin down and cook for 2 minutes. Add the scallops to sear, and turn the fillet on the other side.

While it is cooking, take the mashed potatoes, along with pesto, and heat them quickly. Once done, place the mashed potatoes in the middle of a plate.

Place the snapper, skin up, on top and place the coulis around.

Garnish with the seared scallops and, if available, some fried basil leaves. Drizzle with olive oil.

Superb with a Castello di Borghese Pinot Noir.

red bar & restaurant

417 New York Avenue
Huntington

New American Cuisine

Hours:
Lunch: Monday - Friday Noon - 3 pm
Dinner: Monday - Thursday 4 pm - 9 pm
Friday, Saturday 4 pm - 11 pm
Sunday 4 pm - 9 pm

Phone: 631-673-0304

www.redrestaurantli.com

NINO ANTUZZI, OWNER
MATTHEW SMITH, CHEF

All Major Credit Cards Accepted

Bold colors and clean lines dominate the design of Red, offering vivacious and sophisticated style. The dining room has cool layers of blue and yellow, contrasting with warm light, mirror reflection and honey wood.

New American cuisine is the focus of Red's menu, with ingredients paying tribute to cultures from around the world. Spices, fine meats and fresh seafood are prepared with attention to world flavors and textures. Mussels scented with lemongrass, Moroccan spiced lamb or simply steak frites satisfy seekers of a fine culinary experience in Huntington.

grilled shell steak with gorgonzola-peppercorn sauce

Serves: 4

**4 16-ounce natural fed
shell steaks from
local butcher**

Sauce
**1 cup full bodied red
table wine
1/2 teaspoon whole
black peppercorns
2 cups veal stock**

**1/4 cup heavy cream
6 ounces Gorgonzola
cheese**

Heat grill to medium high

Sauce
In a medium saucepan, add red wine and peppercorns. Heat over medium heat and reduce by 3/4.

Add veal stock. Cook for 15 minutes.

Add heavy cream. Stir. Remove from heat.

Transfer to blender. Add gorgonzola. Pulse until cheese is well incorporated.

Steaks
Season and rub steaks with salt, fresh ground pepper and olive oil.

Place on grill. Grill each side. (Medium rare: approximately 8 minutes each side.)

Remove from grill. Let steaks sit for 5 minutes before serving.

Add sauce, serve and enjoy.

 A natural with Castello di Borghese Merlot Reserve.

REVERE'S
An American Pub

"A Revolution in Dining"

234 Old Country Road
Mineola

Regional American Cuisine

Phone: 516-741-1776

www.reverespub.com

Bob Romer, Jr. and Jim Walsh, Owners
Maureen Romer, Executive Chef

Reservations accepted for parties of 5 or more

ATTIRE: Casual
Visa, MasterCard, American Express

HOURS:
Lunch
Monday - Friday 11:00 am - 4:00 pm
Dinner
Monday - Friday 4:00 pm - 11:00 pm
Saturday 5:00 pm - 11:00 pm
Sunday 4:00 pm - 9:00 pm
Sunday Brunch Noon - 4:00 pm

Revere's is a family owned and operated restaurant featuring regional American cuisine and Early American ambience. The menu boasts a variety of appetizers such as Newport Portobellos with goat cheese, St. Louis Toasted Ravioli, and Classic Wings. A wide array of entrees ensures something for everyone.

pennsylvania dutch pork chops

Serves: 4

4 pork chops
   (¹/₂ inch thick, boneless
   or on the bone)
¹/₄ teaspoon pepper
¹/₂ teaspoon salt

1 ¹/₂ tablespoons flour
1 ¹/₂ tablespoons oil
2 medium onions
   (sliced thin)

¹/₂ cup dark beer
¹/₂ cup beef broth
1 teaspoon cornstarch

Season pork chops with salt and pepper; coat with flour.

Heat oil in sauté pan, add chops and cook on each side 3 minutes.

Add onions and cook for another 5 minutes, turning chops once.

Remove chops to heated platter.

Add beer and beef broth. Season sauce to taste.

Blend cornstarch with cold water.

Stir into sauce and cook until thickened. Pour sauce over chops to serve.

A superb pairing with Castello di Borghese Cabernet Franc.

San Marco
Ristorante
*Exquisite Northern Italian Cuisine
in an elegant setting*

**658 Motor Parkway
Hauppauge**

NORTHERN ITALIAN CUISINE

Reservations Recommended - 800-510-0088 or 631-273-0088

Orlando Andreani, Owner
Jose Rodrigues, Chef

www.sanmarcoristorante.com

Amex, Visa, Master Card, Diners Club

Hours
Lunch
Monday - Friday 11:30 a.m. - 3:00 p.m.
Dinner
Monday - Thursday 5:00 p.m. - 10:00 p.m.
Friday - Saturday 5:00 p.m. - 11:00 p.m.
Closed Sunday

ATTIRE: Neat

Well established for many years, San Marco is graced with elegance in a romantic atmosphere. Brick arches, beautiful paintings, soft lighting by classic wall sconces, and comfortable seating in banquettes add to the refined beauty. With numerous awards, rave reviews, and an attentive and friendly staff, this creative Italian restaurant is a true culinary beauty with old world charm.

chicken raspberry

Serves: 8

16 3-ounce chicken breasts scaloppine
4 cups regular flour
10 medium size egg whites, beaten

3 cups olive oil, not virgin
Salt and pepper to taste
3 cups red wine vinegar
4 cups raspberry marmalade

1½ cups beef stock (can use bouillon cube)
Fresh raspberries for garnish

Flour each chicken scaloppine both sides and dip in the egg whites, shake off excess and set aside. In a large skillet, heat ¼ of the oil. (Oil must be very hot but not smoking.) Add 4 chicken scaloppine and cook for 3 minutes each side, salt and pepper to taste. Remove scaloppine from skillet and keep warm in the oven. Repeat same procedure for the remaining 12 chicken scaloppine. Discard oil from skillet.

Using same skillet, add raspberry marmalade, vinegar and beef stock. Cook on high, stirring frequently, until sauce reduces to 50% of its original volume (4¼ cups). Add salt and pepper to taste.

Add 8 chicken scaloppine to the skillet with 50% of raspberry sauce and cook at medium heat for 5 minutes, spooning sauce on top several times. Remove from skillet and keep at low heat in the oven. Repeat same procedure with the remaining 8 scaloppine.

Serve hot, garnishing it with fresh raspberries on top.

Castello di Borghese Cabernet Franc Reserve's rich spicy flavor accentuates the superb fruit oriented ingredients in this mouth watering dish.

SAVANNA'S

268 Elm Street, Southampton
Tel: 631-283-0202 / Fax: 631-283-6034

Dinner Daily from 5:30 pm
Brunch Saturday and Sunday 10:00 am to 2:30 pm

Reservations Recommended

All major credit cards accepted

Mr. Howard Gittis, Owner
German Lucarelli and Aldo Alo, Chefs

Housed in Southampton Village Hall, which has been converted and beautifully restored, Savanna's is an elegant place to enjoy an evening. Diners feel transported back in time in the open dining room with French doors that lead out to the patio and rose garden. Outdoor dining on summer nights under the pillared pavilion is always a treat.

The menu features local seafood, exotic game, prime steaks, homemade pasta, and organic produce. The kitchen is complemented with a wood burning oven where all of the restaurant's bread is baked and specialty entrees are roasted.

Savanna's is the perfect choice for superior service and a delight for the senses.

lobster cakes with spicy rémoulade

Serves: 2

For Lobster Cakes
1 medium red pepper, diced fine
1 medium Spanish onion, diced fine
2 cloves garlic, diced fine
2 eggs
4 tablespoons mayonnaise

2 tablespoons mustard
3 tablespoons lemon juice
1 cup breadcrumbs (Japanese)
1 pound lobster meat, chopped fine
Salt and pepper

For Spicy Rémoulade
6 ounce Hellman's mayonnaise
2 ounces capers, chopped fine
1 ounce lemon juice
2 ounces ketchup
1 ounce cayenne pepper
Salt and pepper to taste

In a large bowl add all ingredients for lobster cakes except bread crumbs. Mix well. Mix in breadcrumbs. Let stand for about 30 minutes. Form 2-ounce cakes. Pan sear until golden brown on both sides. Remove from pan to plate.

Mix all ingredients together for spicy rémoulade and use as garnish.

Castello di Borghese Barrel Fermented Chardonnay or Pinot Noir are two perfect choices.

199 Middle Road, Sayville
Tel: 631-567-0033

Dinner:
Sunday - Thursday 5 pm to 10 pm
Friday and Saturday 5 pm to 11 pm

American Express Accepted

Reservations required for parties of 5 or more

Casual Attire

PAMELA RAYMOND/RICHARD STAFFORD, OWNERS
WILLIAM BERGIN, CHEF

With all the charm and comfort of a country inn, the Sayville Inn started out as a local tavern in 1888. Owned and operated by Pamela Raymond and Richard Stafford for the past 18 years, this American Bistro has an eclectic clientele as well as an eclectic menu. From burgers to homemade ravioli to pignoli crusted rack of lamb, Chef William Bergin dishes up both menu staples and upscale daily specials.

Join Pamela and Richard for a friendly and enjoyable evening where Teddy Roosevelt used to come (by horseback) for a drink.

tortilla crusted breast of chicken with avocado, tomato, cilantro & lime

Serves: 4

4 large chicken
   breasts, pounded thin
3 cups finely crushed
   tortilla chips
3 large eggs
2 cups flour

¼ cup vegetable oil
3 ripe avocados, diced
1 small red onion, diced
1 large ripe tomato, diced
¼ cup finely chopped
   cilantro

⅛ cup fresh lime juice
⅛ cup extra-virgin olive
   oil
Salt and pepper

Dip the breasts in flour, then egg, then tortilla chips. Heat oil in a large frying pan.
Fry breasts until cooked through. Transfer to plates. Serve with avocado mixture.

Make Beforehand
In bowl, mix together avocados, onion, tomato, cilantro, lime juice, extra-virgin olive
oil, salt and pepper. Refrigerate until served.

*The perky, spicy tones of Castello di Borghese's Cabernet Franc pair well with
this recipe.*

SOUTHAMPTON PUBLICK HOUSE

40 Bowden Square
Southampton Village

Phone: 631-283-2800
Fax: 631-283-2801

<u>Lunch</u>
Monday - Saturday 11:30 am - 4:00 pm
Sunday Brunch Noon - 3:00 pm
<u>Dinner</u>
Monday - Thursday 5:00 pm - 10:00 pm
Friday and Saturday 5:00 pm - 11:00 pm
Sunday 4:00 pm - 9:00 pm

www.publick.com

DONALD SULLIVAN, OWNER
CARL HOLFELDER, CHEF

The Southampton Publick House was established in July 1996 as the first and only Microbrewery/Restaurant located on the East End of Long Island.

In just a few years its products have earned a solid regional and national reputation for their high quality and uniqueness. The brewery produces an eclectic range of traditional British, German, American, and Belgian style beers. Many of their unique products are sold to over 40 specialty beer bars and restaurants throughout Long Island and New York City.

lager marinated ribeye with golden scalloped potatoes

Serves: 2

2 14-ounce rib eye steaks
3 peeled and thinly sliced
   scalloped potatoes
½ cup golden lager
½ cup heavy cream
1 teaspoon chopped garlic
Pinch of salt and pepper

2 slices Swiss cheese

Beer Marinade
3 garlic cloves
3 shallots
1 cup golden lager
1 ounce kitchen bouquet

1 ounce Worcestershire
   sauce
1 ounce soy sauce
1 cup blended oil

For Scalloped Potatoes
Spread scalloped potatoes evenly in a casserole dish. In a separate bowl, mix cream, ½ cup of beer, garlic and a pinch of salt and pepper. Pour over potatoes and cover with aluminum foil. Bake for 45 minutes or until potatoes are soft. Place Swiss cheese on top and bake for an additional 10 minutes.

For Beer Marinade
In a blender, add garlic, shallots, Worcestershire sauce, 1 cup of beer, kitchen bouquet and soy sauce. Blend. Slowly add oil while blending. Place steaks in marinade for 4 hours. Cook on a grill until desired temperature.

Cabernet Franc is a mouth pleaser so maybe you need a "mug".

Tellers®

An American Chophouse

**605 Main Street
Islip**

www.tellerschophouse.com

631-277-7070

Michael Bohlsen, Owner
Craig Jermin, Chef

Reservations Recommended

Casual Neat Attire

HOURS:
Lunch
Monday - Friday 11:30 am - 2:30 pm
Dinner
Monday - Thursday 5:00 pm - 10 pm
Friday and Saturday 5:00 pm - 11 pm

The dining room is a temple-like shrine to ageless style and elegance, a fittingly dramatic setting for Tellers' incredible cuisine. The 32-foot ceilings and refurbished art deco friezes radiate a majestic air throughout the main dining room, the piece de resistance of this 1927 grand stone bank.

Teller's menu complements the dazzling architecture, featuring American chophouse items and American cuisine selections. The lunch and dinner menus are comprised of outstanding varieties of prime aged steaks and chops, as well as local and regional specialties. To accompany your meal, the award-winning wine list offers a diverse and imaginative selection from two wine cellars, holding over 3,000 bottles of wine. Tellers truly offers a unique, memorable dining experience that you can bank on.

steak au poivre

Serves: up to 18

Au Poivre Sauce
1 pound of beef bits
½ large white onion
¾ can green
**   peppercorns to taste**
3 tablespoons thyme

¼ small red onion,
**   minced**
¼ cup black peppercorns
1 cup heavy cream
5 cups veal stock
1 ounce brandy

Steak Au Poivre
Desired number of steaks,
**   salted and peppered to**
**   taste**
2 ounces poivre sauce per
**   steak**

Au Poivre Sauce
Sauté all ingredients together except the heavy cream, veal stock and brandy.

Deglaze with the brandy.

Add cream and veal stock.

Reduce by ¼ to a sauce consistency.

Steak Au Poivre
Season steaks with salt and pepper and broil to desired temperature.

Serve with 2 ounces of Au Poivre Sauce.

Garnish with watercress. Serve immediately.

Castello di Borghese's Ovation, predominantly a Cabernet Franc with layers of complex flavors, is a perfect partner to this simple recipe.

17 East Main Street
Riverhead

631-208-3151
www.tweedsrestaurant.com

EDWIN F. TUCCIO AND DOROTHY MUMA, OWNERS
JEFFREY TRUJILLO, CHEF

Reservations Recommended / Casual Neat Attire

Hours:
Monday - Saturday 10:00 am - 10:00 pm
Sunday 11:00 am - 9:00 pm

Visa, MasterCard, American Express accepted

Everything Old is New Again…
Tweed's Restaurant and Buffalo Bar in the historic J.J. Sullivan Hotel serves the finest of local food specialties and wines representing the best Long Island vineyards. This landmark location has been lovingly restored to recreate a style of dining more than a century old. Tweed's combines true local flavor with sophisticated cuisine in an atmosphere of comfort, warmth, courtesy, and welcoming familiarity. Don't forget to visit their Buffalo ranch in Riverhead.

braised bison short ribs

Serves: 4

6 pounds of bison short ribs (beef short ribs can be substituted, but bison is lower in fat and cholesterol)
2 cups celery, diced

4 cups onions, diced
2 cups carrots, diced
4 cups red wine
2 quarts beef stock
2 fresh thyme sprigs
1 fresh rosemary sprig

½ cup all purpose flour
¼ cup vegetable oil for searing ribs
Salt and pepper to taste

In a flat bottom pan or casserole, heat oil over moderate heat. Season short ribs with salt and pepper. Add to pan, searing meat (to bring out natural sugars and caramelize) on all sides.

Remove meat once seared, and drain oil.
Add vegetables and sauté until onions are translucent.

Add flour to vegetables, stirring until flour slightly browns.

Add wine and stock. Return short ribs to pan, cover and place in a preheated 350°F oven for about 2 ½ hours, or until fork tender.

Remove ribs from pan, strain sauce. Puree the vegetables, and return them to the sauce (removing herbs). Adjust seasoning.

Serve with noodles or mashed potatoes.

Chef's Note: This dish is a great comfort food. Hearty for a winter meal, yet perfect for a summer barbeque.

Castello di Borghese Cabernet Franc Reserve is the ultimate "comfort food" wine.

DESSERTS

desserts

418 North Country Road, St. James
631-584-2058

Jon and Barbara Manougian, Owners
Jon Manougian, Chef
Barbara Manougian, Pastry Chef

Casual neat attire

Dinner
Tuesday - Saturday from 5pm

Credit Cards: AmEx, MC, Visa

tiramisu

Serves: 6 to 8

1 pound mascarpone
   cheese
10 egg yolks
1¼ cups heavy cream
⅔ cup sugar
4-5 cups espresso

1 tablespoon vanilla
   extract
2 large packages lady
   fingers
   (approximately 48)

Beat sugar, vanilla and egg yolks until light - at least 5 minutes. Whip heavy cream in separate bowl. Whip mascarpone into egg mixture until completely smooth. Whisk in heavy cream by hand.

Spread thin layer of cream mixture on bottom of pan. Lightly soak lady fingers in espresso and layer in pan. Spread thin layer of cream mixture over lady fingers. Repeat layer of lady fingers soaked in espresso. Spread rest of cream mixture on top.

Refrigerate (overnight is best). Dust with cocoa powder when ready to serve.

Makes one 9" x 13" pan or one ½" deep aluminum lasagna pan.

Opulent, with a cherry fruit structure, Castello di Borghese Pinot Noir is smooth and silky.

**93 LARKFIELD ROAD
EAST NORTHPORT**

American Foodhouse

Phone: 631-261-5761

**Anastasia Barbatsoulis, Owner
Nicholas Litterello, Chef/Owner**

Reservations Taken for Parties of 6+

Casual Neat Attire

Visa, MasterCard, American Express

**HOURS:
Monday - Thursday
4:30 pm - 10:00 pm
Friday and Saturday
4:30 pm - 11:00 pm
Sunday
4:30 pm - 9:00 pm**

The owners, inspired by their love of good food, music, and ambience, have created an intimate yet comfortable SoHo feel dining space and a menu offering selections from fried chicken to foie gras. Rated "excellent" by the New York Times in 2004.

blueberry banana soup with lemon sorbet

Serves: 4

1 ½ cups sugar
4 ½ cups water
2 pints blueberries
Zest of 1 lemon
Zest of 1 lime

Zest of 1 orange
1 banana
4 sprigs of fresh mint
1 pint lemon sorbet

Combine water and sugar in a pot and bring just to a simmer. Remove from heat and add 1 ½ pints of blueberries. Place in a blender and once it's cooled, puree. Add all zests, puree again for just a few seconds and chill - (leave in blender top, overnight chilling is best).

To Serve: Add banana to blender with blueberry soup and puree. Pour into 4 dessert bowls or 4 large martini glasses, scoop sorbet in center and garnish with mint sprigs and remaining blueberries.

Chef's Note: This is an easy dish that's great in the summer after dinner. It's cool and refreshing. You can change the sorbet flavor or add more fruit.

Castello di Borghese Allegra-Late Harvest Riesling-melon, tropical fruit, peach and pear tones with apricot influence. A satiny mouth feel for a smooth lingering finish.

Captain Bill's

122 Ocean Avenue, Bay Shore
Phone: 631-665-6262
Fax: 631-665-6293

www.captainbills.com

PETER MCCARTHY AND MICHAEL KORB, OWNERS
KEVIN MCCLELLAN, CHEF

Reservations preferred; walk in visitors always welcome

<u>Lunch</u>
Monday - Saturday 11:30 am - 4:00 pm
<u>Dinner</u>
Monday - Saturday from 5:00 pm
Sunday from 4:00 pm
<u>Sunday Brunch</u>
11:30 am - 2:30 pm

All major credit cards accepted

Enjoy wonderful waterfront bay views and spectacular sunsets over the Great South Bay while dining on fresh daily selection of oysters, lobsters, fin fish, aged steaks, and prime rib.

Celebrate with friends and family during our wonderful Sunday brunch on the harbor, or stop by and enjoy our Friday night happy hour where we feature special drink prices complemented by a buffet of hors d'ouvres.

desserts 152

famous warm fudge cakes

Serves: 8

12 ounces semi-sweet
  chocolate
12 ounces butter
6 eggs yolks
10 tablespoons flour
11 tablespoons sugar

2 additional tablespoons
  butter, melted

Optional garnish
Whipped cream,
  raspberries and
  chocolate syrup

Grease 8 8-ounce cups (ramekins) using melted butter. Dust with 10 tablespoons sugar. Using a double-boiler, melt butter and chocolate. Cool slightly. Whip egg yolks, flour and 1 tablespoon sugar on high speed for 8 minutes. Gently fold egg mixture into chocolate. Fill ramekins ¾ full and refrigerate for a least one hour (may be refrigerated overnight and baked-off as needed). Bake at 350°F for 15 minutes (center will not set). Unmold on plate, garnish and serve.

There is nothing better than warm chocolate paired with Castello di Borghese Pinot Noir.

FREDERICK'S

1117 Walt Whitman Road, Melville
Phone: 631-673-8550
Fax: 631-673-7648

KRISTOPHER WOLFF, CHEF/OWNER

Continental Cuisine

Reservations Recommemded
Casual Attire

Lunch
Monday - Friday 11:30 am - 2:00 pm
Dinner
Monday - Friday 5:00 pm - 9:30 pm
Saturday 5:00 pm - 10:00 pm

Credit Cards: Visa, MC, AmEx, and Diner's

Frederick's restaurant is a family run continental restaurant with outstanding service equally matched with its wonderful menu, celebrating its 25th year.

raspberry crème brulee

Serves: 6

8 egg yolks
1 quart heavy cream
4 ounces granulated sugar
   for mixture

2 teaspoons vanilla extract
1 pint fresh raspberries
1 ½ ounces granulated
   sugar for topping

6 brulee dishes
1 baking sheet tray
Propane torch

Preheat the oven to 300°F.
Combine egg yolks, sugar, heavy cream, and vanilla extract in a large mixing bowl and whisk together.

Pour mixture into the six brulee dishes, then evenly place six raspberries into each dish. Place dishes onto sheet tray, adding water onto the sheet tray, creating a water bath. Place in oven for approximately 25 minutes.

Allow to cool. At this time, the crème brulee can be covered in plastic wrap and stored in the refrigerator for 3 days.

To serve, coat the top of the crème brulee with sugar and caramelize with torch.

Chef's Note: This is a wonderful refreshing recipe that can be prepared 3 days in advance.

My favorite dessert should be paired with my favorite wines: Pinot Noir Reserve or Allegra.

LA PLAGE
RESTAURANT

131 Creek Road, Wading River
Tel: 631-744-9200/ Fax: 631-744-9427

www.laplagerestaurant.com

Wayne R. Wadington III, Owner/Chef

Open 7 Days
Lunch: Noon - 3:00 pm
Dinner: 4:00 pm - 10:00 pm

Reservations recommended

Credit cards: Visa, MC, AmEx

Enjoy a romantic dinner at this beachy but elegant hot spot. Sip drinks from a well rounded wine list in the terrace cocktail lounge, then feast on French American eclectic cuisine while overlooking the water. All the food is very fresh and stresses the seasons. The menu changes daily, and fresh fish, both local and from around the globe, is brought in every day. The out-of-the-way trip here will be well worth the hunt.

warm blueberry financier with toasted almond cream & lemon meringue sorbet

Serves: 12

For Blueberry Financier
1 cup flour
1 cup almond flour
1 pound unsalted butter
5 cups confectioners
    sugar
14 egg whites
2 pints blueberries

For Toasted Almond
   Cream
1 quart heavy cream
1 cup sugar
1/2 vanilla bean
1 1/2 cups toasted sliced
    almonds
8 egg yolks

For Lemon Sorbet
1 1/2 cups simple syrup*
12 lemons juiced

For Meringue
6 egg whites
1/4 teaspoon cream of
    tartar
1 1/2 cups confectioners
    sugar

For Blueberry Financier: Melt butter over moderate heat, swirling pan occasionally until butter is a nut brown color. Sift together flour and sugar then add almond flour. Whip egg whites until soft peaks. Then mix in dry ingredients. Slowly pour in brown butter, then fold in blueberries. Bake in 6-ounce buttered and floured ramekins at 375°F until golden brown for about 35 minutes.

For Toasted Almond Cream: Toast almonds very dark. Add sugar, cream, vanilla bean and toasted almonds to a pot and simmer for 20 minutes. Whisk egg yolks until pale. Slowly add hot cream to yolks. Put mixture back on stove on very low heat and stir until it coats the back of a spoon.

For Lemon Sorbet: Mix simple syrup and lemon juice together and freeze according to ice cream machine manufacturer's directions.

For Meringue: Whip egg whites until soft peaks. Slowly add cream of tartar and sugar. Whip on high until firm and shiny.

Presentation: Spoon some toasted almond cream in the middle of each plate. Place financier on sauce. On a separate plate, spoon some meringue over lemon sorbet and caramelize with a blow torch. Top the financier with the sorbet and garnish with fresh mint and confectioners sugar.

Chef's Note: The blueberries can be substituted with any fresh or dried fruit that is available. The lemon meringue sorbet is optional and can be substituted with your favorite ice cream. The financier cakes can be made ahead of time and warmed in a microwave oven.

*Editor's Note: For simple syrup, dissolve sugar in a ratio of 2:1 in water on top of the stove. Let cool completely before using. This can be stored indefinitely in the refrigerator.
A financier is a traditional French cake.

All of the elements of this dessert are in harmony with Castello di Borghese Allegra Late Harvest Riesling.

61 Hill Street, Southampton Village
Tel: 631-283-9323 / Fax: 631-283-9311

Douglas A. Gulija, Chef/Owner

NEW AMERICAN SEAFOOD CUISINE

Dinner is served from 5:30 pm to 11:00 pm, daily, except Mondays
Reservations Recommended

All major credit cards accepted

NEW AMERICAN SEAFOOD CUISINE

In just eight years, the Plaza Café has become a mainstay of fine dining in the Hamptons. The restaurant's quietly elegant ambiance offers a refreshing refuge from the bustling East End summer "scene". Our award-winning cuisine and service are complemented by a world-class wine list with emphasis on American vintages. The Plaza Café has already earned three stars from both the New York Times and Newsday and is listed in Zagat's, "America's Top Restaurants".

vanilla bean roasted pineapple with coconut cake & coconut sorbet (tropical fantasy)

Serves: 4

1 pineapple, peeled
1 vanilla bean, split
1 cup simple syrup
4 coconut cakes
4 tablespoons macadamia
   nuts, chopped
4 dried pineapple
   wedges, for garnish

Coconut Cake
6 ounces butter
8 ounces sugar
3 eggs
1 teaspoon vanilla extract
½ cup cake flour
½ teaspoon baking
   powder

¼ teaspoon salt
5 ounces coconut milk
4 ounces white chocolate,
   melted
5 ounces coconut, toasted
1 quart coconut sorbet
   (available in specialty
   shops)

Place pineapple in sauté pan; pour simple syrup over top, add vanilla bean and roast for approximately 45 minutes in 350°F oven.

Remove pineapple from oven; cool; core and slice into 1 ½ inch slices. Portion slice of pineapple on plate; top with warm coconut cake. Top with coconut sorbet.
Ladle pan juices over for presentation.

Garnish with macadamia nuts and dried pineapple.

Coconut Cake
Butter and flour 10 4-ounce ramekins. Cream butter and sugar. Add eggs and vanilla extract. Sift together the cake flour, baking powder and salt. Add sifted ingredients and coconut milk to mixer. Fold in white chocolate and toasted coconut. Bake at 375°F for 10-12 minutes.

Chef's Note: Simple syrup- combine 1 cup sugar and 1 cup water. Bring to simmer, then remove from heat. Extra coconut cakes can be frozen.

Allegra means happy. This dessert paired with Allegra Late Harvest Riesling will end the meal on a very happy note.

Three Village Inn

150 Main Street
Stony Brook

Phone: 631-751-0555
Fax: 631-751-0593
www.threevillageinn.com

FEATURING CLASSIC AND CONTEMPORARY AMERICAN CUISINE

Joe Taranto, Chef

Hours
Lunch Daily ~ Noon till 4 pm
Dinner Daily ~ From 5 pm
Sunday Brunch ~ 11:30 am - 3 pm
Weekend Breakfast Buffet ~ 8 am - 10 am

All Major Credit Cards Accepted

Enjoy impeccable service in an exquisite setting overlooking scenic Stony Brook Harbor. The seasonal menus have been carefully planned to include classic and contemporary American favorites, along with the freshest Long Island seafood and New England specialties to please the most discriminating palette.

In addition to the Inn's 26 guest rooms, they can also accommodate private parties and weddings in their newly remodeled banquet rooms.

pumpkin dutch apple pie

Serves: 8

¾ cup sugar
2 teaspoons all-purpose
   flour
1 teaspoon lemon juice
1 teaspoon ground
   cinnamon
Dash nutmeg
2 medium apples, peeled,
   cored and chopped
   (about 2 cups)

1½ cups canned
   pumpkin
2 tablespoons butter,
   melted
¼ teaspoon ground
   nutmeg
¼ teaspoon salt
2 eggs
1 cup evaporated milk

Pastry for single-crust
   pie

For Crumb Topping
½ cup all-purpose flour
⅓ cup sugar
⅓ cup chopped nuts
3 tablespoons butter

Combine ¼ cup of the sugar, flour, lemon juice, ¼ teaspoon of the cinnamon and a dash of nutmeg. Add apples; toss to coat fruit. Transfer to a pastry-lined 9-inch pie plate. Set aside.

Combine pumpkin, remaining ½ cup of sugar, melted butter, remaining ¾ teaspoon of cinnamon, ¼ teaspoon nutmeg and salt. Add eggs. Beat lightly with a rotary beater or fork. Gradually stir in evaporated milk. Mix well. Place pie plate with apples on oven rack; pour pumpkin filling on top of apples. Bake in a 375°F oven for 30 minutes.

Combine ingredients for crumb topping and sprinkle over pie. Bake 25-30 minutes more. Cool on a wire rack. Chill, covered.

Allegra is the perfect ending to your wonderful dinner.

ABOUT THE SUFFOLK CHAPTER
ASSOCIATION FOR THE HELP OF RETARDED CHILDREN

Suffolk AHRC is one of the largest voluntary agencies in Suffolk County, with a 55 year tradition of enriching the lives of children and adults with developmental challenges and offering support for their families. Currently, more than 2,500 people benefit from our comprehensive day and residential programs and services.

The Saul & Elaine Seiff Educare Center is a school for children from infancy through age twenty-one. School-age children are enrolled in this program because they have unique needs and challenges which cannot be accommodated through their local school districts. Through our Early Intervention and Pre-School programs, services for "at risk" youngsters often diminish, if not eliminate, the need for costly special services for a lifetime.

Our Vocational Training Program offers adults real work experience at AHRC on-premise Work Centers. Corporations, large and small, outsource packaging and assembly jobs to this program. These contracts provide men and women with opportunities to learn a variety of vocational skills that can ultimately lead to competitive employment.

AHRC's for-profit nursery, Flowerfield Gardens in Holtsville, NY is a garden center that includes 10 cultivation greenhouses and a retail store. The nursery is open to the public and specializes in wholesale and corporate orders. It also offers individuals from the Work Centers a unique off-site vocational experience. They take great pride in seeing the seedlings they cultivate sold to the public as mature and beautiful plants.

Through a unique employment service called Supported Work, adults are carefully matched with businesses by skill level and work setting. Specially trained job coaches facilitate the transition from an AHRC Work Center to a new job. These coaches provide on-the-job training at the employer's site and continuous follow along services.

For those men and women who are not ready for vocational training, AHRC offers a Day Habilitation Program. Here they learn the skills necessary to pursue personal interests and life goals. Satisfying and rewarding connections in the community are available and encouraged. In addition, clinical services are provided where needed.

Our Senior Day Habilitation Program offers meaningful and functional activities that encourage older participants to maintain and even enhance their quality of life.

Nothing eases the concerns of aging parents more than seeing their son or daughter comfortably and safely situated in an AHRC operated residence.

Currently, more than twenty-seven Community Residences are homes to six to eight adults. Each home operates as a family unit, under the supervision and guidance of an AHRC house-parenting team. Residents interact with their communities as typical families do: shopping, banking, visiting the library, going to work. For people requiring on-premise medical attention, three Intermediate Care Facilities offer twenty-four hour nursing.

Suffolk AHRC is overseen by a voluntary Board of Directors comprised mostly of parents and siblings of program participants. The chapter is administered by an executive director, who oversees a staff of 1,000 full and part time employees throughout its 35 locations. It is a chapter of NYSARC, Inc., a family-based organization working with and for people who have mental retardation or other developmental disabilities.

Voluntary contributions are encouraged and appreciated to supplement government funding.

INDEX

Cranberry
Goat Cheese Salad with Sun Dried Cranberries, Brandied
        Pecans & Crumbled Goat Cheese, 53
Grilled Chicken with Apple and Brie Salad with
        Cranberry Vinaigrette, 49

Crème Brulee (See Desserts)

Crostini
Eggplant Caponata with Crostini, 15
Mushroom Tapenade with Crostini, 19

Desserts

Blueberry Banana Soup with Lemon Sorbet, 151
Warm Blueberry Financier with Toasted
        Almond Cream & Lemon Meringue Sorbet, 157
Famous Warm Fudge Cakes, 153
Pumpkin Dutch Apple Pie, 161
Raspberry Crème Brulee, 155
Tiramisu, 149
Vanilla Bean Roasted Pineapple with Coconut Cake
        & Coconut Sorbet, 159

Eggplant

Eggplant Caponata with Crostini, 15
Eggplant Napoleon, 35

Endive
Watercress Endive Salad with Bleu Cheese, Pink Grapefruit,
        Garlic Chips, & Champagne Vinaigrette, 47

Entrees
Blackened Fluke with Cheese Grits & Greens, 95
Braised Bison Short Ribs, 143
Brandade de Morue (Cod Fish Soufflé), 87
Butter Poached Maine Lobster & Monk Fish Loin with
        Julienne Vegetables & Mustard Spaetzle, 99
Chicken Mediterranean, 85
Chicken Michelangelo, 123
Chicken Raspberry, 133
Chilean Sea Bass Alla Lucia, 121
Filet Mignon Medallions with Sliced Shiitake Mushroom
        Port Wine Demi Glaze, 105
Grilled Chicken & Arugula Salad with Roasted Red
        Pepper-Balsamic Vinaigrette, 91
Grilled Shell Steak with Gorgonzola-Peppercorn Sauce, 129
Horseradish Crusted Salmon Filets, 93
Lager Marinated Rib Eye with Golden
        Scalloped Potatoes, 139
Lawand Chicken Breast with Chef's Rich, Special Gravy, 117
Lobster Cakes with Spicy Remoulade, 135
Lobster Meat in Brodetto over Angel Hair, 119
Lomo Saltado (Jumping Beef Sauté), 83
Macadamia Encrusted Arctic Char Toasted Orzo Pasta, 109
Macadamia-Nut Crusted Salmon with Red Bean Salsa, 115
Pan Seared Scallops and Shrimp with Fricassee of Oyster
        Mushroom & Leeks, 97
Pan Seared Sea Bass with Vegetable Mousaka
        and Tatziki Relish, 81
Pennsylvania Dutch Pork Chops, 131

Porcini Dusted Diver Sea Scallops in a Creole Mustard
        Cream Sauce, 125
Salmon O'Brien, 113
Sautéed Soft Shell Crabs with Brown Hazelnut Butter
        & Ripe Cherry Tomatoes, 107
Seared Red Snapper Served with Basil Mashed Potatoes
        & Roasted Tomato Coulis, 127
Sesame Seared Tuna, 111
Shrimp Scampi, 101
Steak Au Poivre, 141
Tortilla Crusted Breast of Chicken with Avocado, Tomato,
        Cilantro & Lime, 137
Veal Casa Rustica, 103
Venison Osso Buco, 89

Escargot (See Seafood)

Filet, Beef

Filet Mignon Medallions with Sliced Shiitake Mushroom
        Port Wine Demi Glaze, 105
Tar Tar of Filet Mignon, 23

Fish
Blackened Fluke with Cheese Grits & Greens, 95
Brandade De Morue (Cod Fish Souffle), 87
Butter Poached Maine Lobster & Monk Fish Loin with
        Julienne Vegetables & Mustard Spaetzle, 99
Chilean Sea Bass Alla Lucia, 121
Horseradish Crusted Salmon Filets, 93
Macadamia Encrusted Arctic Char Toasted Orzo Pasta, 109
Macadamia-Nut Crusted Salmon with Red Bean Salsa, 115
Pan Seared Sea Bass with Vegetable Mousaka
        and Tatziki Relish, 81
Salmon O'Brien, 113
Sashimi of Salmon, 37
Seared Red Snapper Served with Basil, Mashed Potatoes
        & Roasted Tomato Coulis, 127
Sesame Seared Tuna, 111
Tuna Tartare with Micro Green Salad & Wasabi Ginger
        Lime Vinaigrette, 5

Fluke (See Fish, Seafood)

Fricassee
Pan Seared Scallops and Shrimp with Fricassee of Oyster
        Mushroom and Leeks, 97

Fudge
Famous Warm Fudge Cake, 153

Garlic

Roasted Garlic Crusted Shrimp, 7
Watercress Endive Salad with Bleu Cheese, Pink Grapefruit,
        Garlic Chips & Champagne Vinaigrette, 47

Grapefruit
Watercress Endive Salad with Bleu Cheese, Pink Grapefruit,
        Garlic Chips & Champagne Vinaigrette, 47

Grits
Blackened Fluke with Cheese Grits & Greens, 95

Hazelnut (See Nuts)

Jam

Corn Fried Oysters with Dijon Aioli & Lemon Jam, 11

Leeks

Pan Seared Scallops and Shrimp with Fricassee of Oyster
     Mushroom and Leeks, 97

Lemon
Blueberry Banana Soup with Lemon Sorbet, 151
Warm Blueberry Financier withToasted
     Almond Cream& Lemon Meringue Sorbet , 157

Lentils
Lump Crab Cakes over Lentil Salad with Wasabi Mayo, 31

Lobster (See Seafood, Shellfish)

Macadamia Nuts (See Nuts)

Mango
Curried Diver Scallops with a Mint Mango Coulis, 21
Roasted Diver Sea Scallops with Mangoes, Thai
     Chilies & Cashews, 17

Marinade
Lager Marinated Rib Eye Potatoes with Golden
     Scalloped Potatoes, 139

Mousaka
Pan Seared Sea Bass with Vegetable Mousaka
     & Tatziki Relish, 81

Mushrooms
Filet Mignon Medallions with Sliced Shiitake Mushroom
     Port Wine Demi Glaze, 105
Mozzarella Napoletana, 27
Mushroom Risotto, 67
Mushroom Tapenade with Crostini, 19
Pan Seared Scallops and Shrimp with Fricassee of Oyster
     Mushroom and Leeks, 97
Porcini Dusted Diver Sea Scallops in a Creole Mustard
     Cream Sauce, 125
Portobello Nape, 13

Nuts

Goat Cheese Salad with Sun Dried Cranberries, Brandied
     Pecans & Crumbled Goat Cheese, 53
Macadamia Encrusted Arctic Char Toasted Orzo Pasta, 109
Macadamia-Nut Crusted Salmon with Red Bean Salsa, 115
Roasted Diver Sea Scallops with Mangoes, Thai
     Chilies & Cashews, 17

Sautéed Soft Shell Crabs with Brown Hazelnut Butter
     & Ripe Cherry Tomatoes, 107
Warm Blueberry Financier with Toasted Almond Cream &
     Lemon Meringue Sorbet, 157
Warm Pears & Gorgonzola Salad, 51

Orzo

Macadamia Encrusted Arctic Char Toasted Orzo Pasta, 109

Osso Buco
Venison Osso Buco, 89

Oysters (See Seafood, Shellfish)

Pasta

Lobster Meat in Brodetto over Angel Hair (pasta), 119
Macadamia Encrusted Arctic Char Toasted Orzo Pasta, 109
Pasta Veal Ragu, 65
Penne ala Vodka, 69
Penne's From Heaven, 75
Rigatoni with Shrimp, Spinach & Goat Cheese, 71
Spaghetti or Vermicelli in Clam Sauce, 73

Pear
Warm Pears & Gorgonzola Salad, 51

Pecans (See Nuts)

Pie
Pumpkin Dutch Apple Pie, 161

Pineapple
Vanilla Bean Roasted Pineapple with Coconut Cake
     & Coconut Sorbet, 159

Pork
Pennsylvania Dutch Pork Chops, 131

Potatoes
Lager Marinated Rib Eye with Golden
     Scalloped Potatoes, 139
Seared Red Snapper Served with Basil Mashed Potatoes
     & Roasted Tomato Coulis, 127

Pumpkin
Pumpkin Dutch Apple Pie, 161

Raspberry

Chicken Raspberry, 133
Raspberry Crème Brulee, 155

Red Snapper (See Fish, Seafood)

Relish
Pan Seared Sea Bass with Vegetable Mousaka
     & Tatziki Relish, 81

Remoulade
Lobster Cakes with Spicy Remoulade, 135

Risotto
Lobster Risotto, 63
Mushroom Risotto, 67

Salad

Bella Vita City Grill's Famous House Chopped Salad, 45
Chilled Maine Lobster Salad with Asparagus in 25 year
    old Balsamic Vinegar, 43
Goat Cheese Salad with Sun Dried Cranberries, Brandied
    Pecans & Crumbled Goat Cheese, 53
Grilled Chicken & Arugula Salad with Roasted Red Pepper
    Balsamic Vinaigrette, 91
Grilled Chicken with Apples and Brie Salad with
    Cranberry Vinaigrette, 49
Lump Crab Cakes over Lentil Salad with Wasabi Mayo, 31
Tuna Tartare with Micro Green Salad & Wasabi Ginger
    Lime Vinaigrette, 5
Warm Pears & Gorgonzola Salad, 51
Watercress Endive Salad with Bleu Cheese, Pink Grapefruit,
    Garlic Chips & Champagne Vinaigrette, 47

Salmon (See Fish, Seafood)

Salsa
Macadamia-Nut Crusted Salmon with Red Bean Salsa, 115

Sauce
Grilled Shell Steak with Gorgonzola-Peppercorn Sauce, 129
Lobster Cakes with Spicy Remolade, 135
Pacific Wonton Wrapped Shrimp with Ponzu Wasabi
    Dipping Sauce, 29
Porcini Dusted Diver Sea Scallops in a Creole Mustard
    Cream Sauce, 125
Spaghetti or Vermicelli in Clam Sauce, 73
Steak Au Poivre, 141

Scallops (See Seafood, Shellfish)

Seafood
  Arctic Char
    Macadamia Encrusted Arctic Char Toasted
      Orzo Pasta, 109
  Cod Fish
    Brandade de Morue (Cod Fish Soufflé), 87
  Crab
    Lump Crab Cakes over Lentil Salad
      with Wasabi Mayo, 31
    Sautéed Soft Shell Crabs with Brown Hazelnut Butter
      & Ripe Cherry Tomatoes, 107
  Escargots
    Escargots Bourguignons, 25
  Fluke
    Blackened Fluke with Cheese Grits & Greens, 95
  Lobster
    Butter Poached Maine Lobster & Monk Fish Loin
      with Julienne Vegetables & Mustard Spaetzle, 99
    Chilled Maine Lobster Salad with Asparagus in
      25 year old Balsamic Vinegar, 43
    Lobster Cakes with Spicy Remoulade, 135
    Lobster Meat in Brodetto over Angel Hair, 119
    Lobster Spring Rolls, 33
    Sherried Lobster Bisque, 55

Oysters
    Corn Fried Oysters with Dijon Aioli & Lemon Jam, 11
Red Snapper
    Seared Red Snapper Served with Basil Mashed
      Potatoes & Roasted Tomato Coulis, 127
Salmon
    Horseradish Crusted Salmon Filets, 93
    Macadamia-Nut Crusted Salmon with Red
      Bean Salsa, 115
    Salmon O'Brien, 113
    Sashimi of Salmon, 37
Sea Bass
    Chilean Sea Bass Alla Lucia, 121
    Pan Seared Sea Bass with Vegetable Mousaka &
      Tatziki Relish, 81
Scallops
    Curried Diver Scallops with a Mint Mango Coulis, 21
    Pan Seared Scallops and Shrimp with Fricassee of
      Oyster Mushroom and Leeks, 97
    Porcini Dusted Diver Sea Scallops in a Creole
      Mustard Cream Sauce, 125
    Roasted Diver Sea Scallops with Mangoes, Thai
      Chilies, & Cashews, 17
Shrimp
    Pacific Wonton Wrapped Shrimp with Ponzu Wasabi
      Dipping Sauce, 29
    Pan Seared Scallops & Shrimp with Fricassee of
      Oyster Mushroom & Leeks, 97
    Rigatoni with Shrimp, Spinach & Goat Cheese, 71
    Roasted Garlic Crusted Shrimp, 7
    Shrimp Scampi, 101
Tuna
    Tuna Tartare with Micro Green Salad & Wasabi
      Ginger Lime Vinaigrette, 5

Sesame
Sesame Seared Tuna, 111

Shell Fish
Butter Poached Maine Lobster & Monk Fish Loin with
    Julienne Vegetables & Mustard Spaetzle, 99
Chilled Maine Lobster Salad with Asparagus in 25 year
    old Balsamic Vinegar, 43
Corn Fried Oysters with Dijon Aioli & Lemon Jam, 11
Curried Diver Scallops with a Mint Mango Coulis, 21
Lobster Cakes with Spicy Remoulade, 135
Lobster Meat in Brodetto over Angel Hair, 119
Lobster Spring Rolls, 33
Lump Crab Cakes over Lentil Salad
    with Wasabi Mayo, 31
Pacific Wonton Wrapped Shrimp with Ponzu Wasabi
    Dipping Sauce, 29
Pan Seared Scallops and Shrimp with Fricassee of Oyster
    Mushroom and Leeks, 97
Porcini Dusted Diver Sea Scallops in a Creole Mustard
    Cream Sauce, 125
Rigatoni with Shrimp, Spinach & Goat Cheese, 71
Roasted Diver Sea Scallops with Mangoes, Thai
    Chilies, & Cashews, 17
Roasted Garlic Crusted Shrimp, 7
Sautéed Soft Shell Crabs with Brown Hazelnut Butter
    & Ripe Cherry Tomatoes, 107
Sherried Lobster Bisque, 55

notes